YO-ABN-098

Leadership
Challenges for Today's Manager

Leadership
Challenges for Today's Manager

Robert L. Taylor
and
William E. Rosenbach

With a foreword by
David Campbell

NICHOLS PUBLISHING/NEW YORK
McGRAW-HILL BOOK COMPANY/LONDON

First published in 1989 by Nichols Publishing,
P.O. Box 96, New York, NY 10024

Books bearing the Nichols Publishing imprint are
published by GP Publishing, Inc.

Library of Congress Cataloging-in-Publication Data

Rosenbach: William E.
      Leadership: challenges for today's manager /
William E. Rosenbach and Robert L. Taylor
      p. cm.
      ISBN 0-89397-317-3
      1. Leadership.   I. Taylor, Robert L.
      (Robert Lewis), 1939-
II. Title.
HD57.7.R67 1988
658.4'092—dc19   88-22361
                                                 CIP

Published in the United Kingdom by McGraw-Hill
Book Company (UK) Limited, Shoppenhangers Road,
Maidenhead, Berkshire, England SL6 2QL

British Library Cataloguing in Publication Data
Taylor, Robert L. 1939-
      Leadership: Challenges for Today's Manager
1.Business firms. Management. Leadership.
I. Title.   II. Rosenbach, William E.
658.4'092
ISBN 0-07-707160-3

This book is dedicated to Ed Johnson and Ballard Morton. By example and inspiration, they demonstrate the finest qualities of executive leadership.

CONTENTS

PART 1—EXPECTATIONS FOR LEADERSHIP, 1

1. Wanted: Corporate Leaders, *Walter Kiechel III*, 7

2. The Antileadership Vaccine, *John W. Gardner*, 13

3. How Do Leaders Get to Lead?, *Michael M. Lombardo*, 22

PART 2—THE CORE INGREDIENTS, 29

4. The Manager: Master and Servant of Power, *Fernando Bartolomé*, and *André Laurent*, 35

5. The Visionary Leader, *Marshall Sashkin*, 45

6. Entrepreneurial Managers in Large Organizations, *Richard Molz*, 53

7. High Hurdles: The Challenge of Executive Self-Development, *Robert E. Kaplan, Wilfred H. Drath*, and *Joan R. Kofodimos*, 61

PART 3—STYLE AND SUBSTANCE, 81

8. The Case for Directive Leadership, *Jan P. Muczyk* and *Bernard C. Reimann*, 89

9. Leadership: More Doing Than Dash, *Peter F. Drucker*, 109

10. Leadership: Good, Better, Best, *Bernard M. Bass*, 112

11. Dancing on the Glass Ceiling, *Regina E. Herzlinger*, 130

12. Qualities of a Successful CEO, *Thomas R. Horton*, 134

PART 4—THE WORLD AROUND US: PAST, PRESENT, AND FUTURE, 143

13. Lessons from Literature, *Ken Kovacs*, 149

14. Plato: Philosopher-Manager, *John K. Clemens* and *Douglas F. Mayer*, 154

15. Bach to Basics, *Charles Smith*, 165

16. The Two Cultures in Business Education, *Thomas M. Mulligan*, 170

PART 5—THE IMPERATIVES OF VALUES AND ETHICS, 181

17. Shaping Business Values, *Thomas R. Horton*, 187

18. Ethical Managers Make Their Own Rules, *Sir Adrian Cadbury*, 191

19. The Hollow Executive, *Robert D. Gilbreath*, 200

FOREWORD

Leadership is an elusive concept, tinged with irony, ringed with paradoxes, and spiced with relevance.

The irony includes the realization that leadership requires a public forcefulness, a certainty of stated purpose, when there has never been a nonpathological leader alive who has not laid awake late at night, listening to the creaks and groans of the palace settling down after a critical day, thinking, "I am determined to do the right thing for my people . . . I wonder what that is?"

The paradoxes range through the developmental to the legal to the ethical. For example, no one is capable of leading very many very far very long without first undergoing a long apprenticeship of successful followership. Leadership requires all the usually recognized qualities of vision, charisma, and integrity, plus an intimate knowledge of the nuts-and-bolts of the operation. No one is going to turn the farm over to you until you have demonstrated the ability to plow straight furrows for days on end. Plowing straight furrows may have little to do with the actual task of leadership once you are in office, but it has everything to do with getting there in the first place.

The ethical paradoxes of leadership are particularly poignant. What do you do as chief executive officer in a drug manufacturing concern, when confronted with the following dilemma: The government rushes to you in the face of a predicted flu epidemic and says, "We need ten million doses of flu vaccine, and we expect you, as responsible corporate citizens, to produce them in a hurry. Your country needs your help to prevent a possible public health disaster. In the interests of urgency, we will pay you cost plus 10 percent."

So far, so good.

Then your legal and statistical staff tells you, "Working from the inadequate data that we have, we estimate that the injection of ten million doses of vaccine will probably produce X cases of severe side effects; of these, some subset Y will surely sue us, and of those litigants, some subset Z may win settlements of size \$A. Using our most conventional estimates, our 'best case' estimate of \$A is roughly equal to last year's earnings. Of course, any of the X, Y, or Z factors could be off either direction by a factor of 10. Our 'worst case' estimate is that this project could bankrupt the company many times over." You are a leader and a responsible citizen; are you going to bet the company?

Or as a military leader, how do you handle the philosophical paradox as a God-fearing citizen who believes in the biblical injunction "Thou Shall Not Kill" when it conflicts with your solemn commissioning oath "to support and defend the Constitution of the United States against all enemies, foreign and domestic." What do you do when placed in a position where defending the Constitution, which incidentally guarantees you the freedom to follow your religious principles, requires you to unleash lethal firepower against opposing forces who intend to deny you the right to practice your beliefs, which include "Thou Shall Not Kill?"

Or how do you handle the paradoxical application of integrity when, as a leader, you are sent in to take over a failing manufacturing plant and find that if you can only keep body and soul together for sixty days, you have a pretty good chance of landing a lucrative contract that will get you out of the woods, pay off your creditors, and provide continuous employment to your work force. But if you level with your people and tell them they may be out of a job in sixty days, that information made public will surely chase away your vendors, dry up your bank line-of-credit loans, and drive away your most talented employees, thereby guaranteeing failure. What does integrity mean in a situation where a deliberate lie seems to be the only route to a noble outcome?

The fact that these paradoxes seem so real and intense is in itself evidence of the relevancy of leadership. Leadership is where the action is. It is bright orange, there is nothing gray about it (except of course the early interminable mindless ploughing of the furrows). To be in charge means to be alive, to unleash your own personal potential, to be able to watch your ideas blossom, to escape Thoreau's life of "quiet desperation." To lead is to be.

DAVID CAMPBELL, PH.D.

PREFACE

Leadership is *the* topic of interest in an increasingly complex, multi-cultural world. There seem to be growing numbers of books on leaders, prescriptions for leadership, and critiques of organizations.
Situations are analyzed for success and failure of the person in charge.
We are faced with simultaneous simplicity and complexity.

To many, there are not enough true leaders. They lament that too few men and women are willing to take charge and provide us with effective leadership. Our current state of the world is defined as an absence of leadership; all we need are a few good leaders. Is it really that simple?

For all the studies, case histories, and experiments, we still know relatively little about the cause and effect of successful leadership. The issues are complex; human personalities, social change, technological innovations, and dynamic organizational environments are linked in strange ways. No two settings, no two individuals combine the same mix of attributes. The result is that we have been unable to isolate leadership as a unitary phenomenon. What do we teach? How can we learn?

Our purpose is to develop a framework for understanding leadership in the context of both the simple and complex perspectives. Having studied nearly two thousand articles written on leadership these past ten years, we find that too few of them have a meaningful message for the person who is living and working in today's organizations. The task was to identify those that speak to the practicing manager. We rejected the "how to" pieces in favor of those that stimulate thought and controversy. These short, introspective articles provide the reader with pieces of a puzzle that can be arranged in his or her own fashion to construct a notion of leadership—one that is individual and meaningful.

Each of the authors expresses himself or herself in a special way. We consciously chose not to write "our" perspective. Rather, our intent is to take the best of what the leading writers present and weave it together into a fabric that stimulates one to think.

After all, leadership depends on one's self-knowledge. If we can help to develop that aspect of leadership potential, it will have more impact than any of the prescriptions offered by the "leader-makers."

This book is written for managers who are "doing" leadership or who aspire to be leaders. We depart from convention because of our experience, our study of leadership *and leaders,* and a conviction that contemporary organizations require multi- and interdisciplinary approaches. Learning from the past, we use the present knowledge and technology to develop a vision of the future.

We see leaders as people who make things happen. Leadership is hard work and sometimes disappointing. It is also challenging and exciting—an adventure. Most of all, effective leadership is fun!

The articles we selected reflect difficult choices. We accepted that responsibility with full knowledge that some good essays were not included. The task was one that we accomplished with a commitment to the continued study of leadership. Our work was made much easier with the professional assistance of Leesa Foster and Marda Numann. We give them our special thanks for their energy and enthusiasm.

Now, you have it. We see a variety of complex factors in the leadership dimension. Each part of the book is dedicated to exploring those factors as they relate to individual action. We leave it to you, the reader, to develop the self-knowledge necessary to understand your own leadership potential.

PART 1
EXPECTATIONS FOR
LEADERSHIP

Leadership is a topic of continuing interest and debate. We are grateful for good leadership; anything less is criticized and often rejected. Yet, as our lives become more complex, there is an increasing frustration that there are too few true leaders.

The study of leadership has become intense in recent years. Researchers are trying to determine the causes and effects of successful leadership. Popular writers are producing volumes that attempt to provide narrative descriptions of leadership using case studies. Many people are searching for a set of prescriptive activities and leader behaviors.

But the more we study, the less we really seem to know. More than ever it seems, there are too few leaders to cope with the opportunities and challenges we face. Have we exhausted the supply of leaders? Has our technological world made the task of leadership an impossible one? Perhaps nothing has really changed. Perhaps we are simply more aware now of our leaders and their impact on our lives.

What Is It That We Want?

Incredibly high expectations are set for leaders today. Study the position description for the top jobs in public and private organizations. You will find that these leadership roles are defined in such a way that few people can possibly respond. Leaders are expected to take charge, set and sometimes fulfill nearly impossible goals, be innovative, perform magic with budgets, maintain harmony with all constituencies, and keep everyone satisfied with their jobs. There is also the sense that leaders must anticipate changes in the internal and external environments, develop responses to those changes, and always be successful. The short run is critical to shareholders, while the long run is essential to an organization's survival. Leaders are asked to give full attention to both.

Communications technology gives us immediate access to our leaders. More than ever, the leader is visible and under constant scrutiny. History is recorded as it happens. No mistake or achievement need go unnoticed. More importantly, we seem to make "news" out of every foible so that leaders must not only think about the task, they must also pay close attention to how they will be perceived by the ever-present media. In a sense, the leader can never leave the stage. This reduces the chance that leaders will attempt the bold actions that could possibly result in failure as well as success.

Followership also presents a dilemma to the leader. Whether leadership rests in a single individual or with the group, how we *respond* often causes problems. Because we know so much about the leader and what he or she does (and does not do), there is a growing tendency for organization members to critique leader effectiveness. The fact is that we do not set expectations for ourselves in responding responsibly to the leader. Even when an apparent consensus is reached, organization members are not reluctant to act independently. Thus, the leader is left with a constituency that resists his or her call to action. The real challenge is to define the role for those to be led and build a commitment to achieve common goals.

The nature of leadership in modern society is constantly changing. Many people are still willing to serve as leaders, but we are more selective in choosing them now. Their past activities and present actions are subject to the closest scrutiny. Our performance expectations are high, and we do not react well to those who do not meet them.

The Changing Environment of Organizations

Corporate leadership is global in scope. There are a variety of multicultural and cross-cultural issues to be addressed. This diversity adds new dimensions to leadership, many of which we are just discovering.

Technology is changing leadership as well. Corporate leadership has traditionally been associated with human capital. But as machines replace production workers and computers take over many of the staff functions, knowledge and information are rapidly becoming the necessary tools of the leader. Bold actions are often discussed in financial terms. Details of day-to-day activities are available to the CEO on a real-time basis. Options can be analyzed, decisions executed, and feedback received with lightning speed and efficiency. Leader effectiveness can be reduced to split-second timing. Technology is both a blessing and a curse to leadership.

One thing is clear. Leadership depends more and more on the acquisition, analysis, and communication of information. Such skills do not depend a great deal on intellect, but education is important. There is the very real possibility that leadership will once again be reserved for an elite—those with a superior education that is well rounded and broadly based.

Evolution in business continues. The environment is more ambiguous and complex. This rapidly changing environment affects the opportunities for and the arena of leadership.

Executive Roles

Administrators, managers, and leaders are all associated with the role of an executive. Over the years there have been many debates about leadership and management. Some people see them as the same. Others fervently believe that they are different. We take the position that such discussions are not productive. Whether leadership and management are alike or different is up to you.

A helpful way to define management is to see it as a set of functions, most commonly accepted as planning, organizing, and controlling. These functions can be taught and learned. The resources involved are people, money, materials, information, and time. Effective management involves the planning, organizing, and controlling of these resources in pursuit of organizational objectives. Thus, there are many tools and techniques that a skillful manager may employ through a combination of education and experience.

Leadership, then, can be described as an influence process. The end result is defined in terms of the organizational objectives. Certainly, effective leaders are skilled in working with people to accomplish those objectives. Specific methods are not well defined because influence is a product of personality interactions. There are still questions as to whether one can be educated or trained to be a leader, but we suggest that people can *learn* to be effective leaders.

Managers do not necessarily lead. In some cases, effective leaders have not been good managers. However, we find that successful leadership and good management go hand in hand. The best business leaders have also distinguished themselves as superb managers. The common elements are more important than any debates about the differences.

Leadership Perspectives

The first step in understanding leadership is to develop a perspective that relates to the world of business that is evolving. Men and women aspiring to leadership roles need to have a model as they think about their own personal strengths and shortcomings. The three selections that follow provide some interesting approaches to understanding leadership.

William Kiechel articulates the need in "Wanted: Corporate Leaders." In this piece, the theme of leadership as a psychological phenomenon is presented. The dilemma of what we expect of leaders today is presented in the second article, "The Antileadership Vaccine," by John Gardner. This is a classic discussion of the issues we face in the challenges and opportunities of the future as well as a rationale for an apparent lack of enthusiasm for leadership by young people today. Finally, Michael Lombardo's "How Do Leaders Get to Lead?" suggests that we may not nurture leadership in a responsible way because of organizational structure and policies.

What is leadership? What do we want it to be? Are we up to the challenge? These are the questions that must be answered if we are to have proper expectations of our leaders.

1
WANTED:
CORPORATE LEADERS

Walter Kiechel III

It's in the air, trend spotters, just about ready to precipitate in the swirling clouds of economic change and rain down on us in a thousand articles and speeches. It's behind much of the business community's fascination with Lee Iacocca. It has something to do with why *In Search of Excellence*, a study of what authors Thomas J. Peters and Robert H. Waterman, Jr., describe as America's best-run companies, has sold over 300,000 copies and became a No. 1 best-seller nationwide. It's there just below the surface of all the talk about fostering entrepreneurialism inside the large corporation.

This soon to be very hot subject is leadership.

At the mere mention of the word, your eyes might reasonably glaze over, iced with recollection of too many politicians promising a new tomorrow, too many unread books with the big L in the title, too many after-dinner exhortations by football coaches who should never have been permitted to doff their windbreakers and eschew their gum. Wake up. This time there may actually be something there.

Item: In an interview a young associate professor at one of those ultra-prestigious business schools announces that when he completes his latest tome on corporate strategy—a bandwagon he's been riding for five years—he proposes to devote himself full-time to the study of leadership. And where will he begin his research? "The military academies," he replies.

Item: Executive recruiters, asked what qualities their client companies are seeking in a candidate for a top job, report that they're hearing our old friend "charisma" a great deal more than they used to. "Vision" also seems in increasing demand; while the headhunters aren't sure precisely what the term means, they sense that it has to do with new and much-sought after skills in motivating people.

Item: In 1981 Matsushita Electric Industrial Co. endowed a chair in leadership at the Harvard Business School—the first professorship devoted to the subject to be established at any major business school. In preparing students to deal with the flesh-and-blood variable in the business equation, these institutions have traditionally taught organizational design, human behavior in different organizational contexts, maybe a bit of labor relations—the skills, in short, that would be called on in planning and administering a bureaucracy.

In February [1983], after casting about hither and yon for an expert on leadership, Harvard awarded the Matsushita professorship to Abraham Zaleznik, already the holder of another endowed chair at HBS and one of the faculty members who had helped raise the money from the Japanese company. Zaleznik, a lay psychoanalyst with a private practice he conducts from beside a couch in his campus office, is the author of an award-winning 1977 article arguing that the psychology of leaders differs dramatically from that of managers. The article raised the hackles of many of Zaleznik's colleagues at the institution formally named the Graduate School of Business Administration.

Most of the interesting thinking about leadership these days—and the punch such thinking has, way beyond the usual pep-rally bromides—has its roots in this notion that psychologically, managers and leaders are very different cups of tea indeed. Zaleznik claims no monopoly on the idea. He sees it reflected, for example, in the distinction James MacGregor Burns makes in his book *Leadership* between transformative leaders, who change the course of events, and transactional ones, who without much emotional involvement get things done through contractual relationships within some sort of organizational structure. Other academics trace the idea back to sociologist Max Weber, who argued that charismatic leaders launch enterprises, only to give way to bureaucrats who take over the running of them.

The experts who of late seem to make the most sense of the leader-manager distinction are (hold on to your hats and your prejudices) Freudians—men like Zaleznik and Harry Levinson, the Menninger Foundation–trained psychologist whose Levinson Institute seminars are perhaps the only forum that routinely brings together businessmen and clinicians. The title of Levinson's seminar for corporate officers is, and has been for 14 years, "On Leadership."

Just more psychohumbug? It may seem to the casual observer that the Freudians are on the run, pilloried in everything from trendy books such as *Psychoanalysis: The Impossible Profession* to movies—the recent "Lovesick," for example, in which Dudley Moore plays an analyst caught up in the toils of counter-transference (that is, he falls in love with a patient). Ach, the followers of Sigmund rejoin, you have to distinguish between our underlying theory and our therapeutic techniques. Did any other theory survive the new-therapies-and-psychobabble explosion of the 1960s and 1970s with as much of its explanatory and predictive power intact?

Much of Freudian doctrine, you may recall from the psychology course you took in college to buck up your average, revolves around a sort of tripartite division of the psyche—into id, ego, and superego. According to the Freudians, it is the particular and characteristic way that these three act and interact within the leader that sets him apart from others, including the manager. Recognizing how these psychodynamics work and consciously trying to ape some of the resultant behavior may even make your own bureaucratic style more inspiring.

In just about everyone, the theory goes, the id is a bubbling, seething stew of instinctual energies, often energies of the randiest or most aggressive sort, all of which in a civilized person are usually kept unconscious. The superego, by contrast, incorporates what our parents and society have taught us about being good; it rewards us psychically for a job well done and also bestows that attribute essential to middle-class life, a sense of guilt. Finally, there's the ego, largely conscious and always caught up in mediating between the other two parts and outside reality. Thus, in Freudian theory, "Man is basically a battlefield," in the felicitous words of the British psychologist Donald Bannister, "a dark cellar in which a well-bred spinster lady and a sex-crazed monkey are forever engaged in mortal combat, the struggle being refereed by a rather nervous bank clerk."

For the leader, though, the internal struggle seems in some ways less bitter, less divisive. In him, the psychologists speculate, that harsh, nagging component of the superego that we commonly call the conscience isn't quite as punitive as it is in other folks. This lets him more readily admit into consciousness the impressions, energies, and associations that bubble up from the id. Asked for his definition of vision, Zaleznik replies, "It's the capacity to see connections, to draw inferences that aren't obvious, that are unprecedented." Some businessmen call it the ability to see around corners as the leader peers into his company's future. It's a talent that has come to seem all the more valuable as the pace of technological and economic change quickens.

This isn't the only element in the leader's vision, however. Perhaps because he has less energy invested in the conscience, he channels more into another component of the superego, the ego ideal. The ego ideal is the image of what he wants himself, and by extension his organization, to be. This vision, which he strives constantly to achieve, is perhaps the most powerful motivational tool in the leader's kit. It gives him a consistent sense of who he is and what he's after, a sense that he can, by words and example, invite others to share in.

As Harry Levinson parses the psychodynamics at work, the leader's pursuit of an ego ideal enables him to frame a transcendent purpose for his organization. (Zaleznik prefers the slightly less highfalutin formulation "enduring goal.") This purpose usually includes within it the perpetuation of the organization, and hence necessarily entails taking a long-term view. Since merely staying alive isn't by itself all that beckoning an ideal, the transcendent purpose will commonly be cast in more inspiring terms—making the best computers in the world, say, or the best cars.

While your typical manager-bureaucrat tries to get people to do things for money or out of fear, the leader invites his co-workers to identify their pursuit of an ego ideal with his own, and with the transcendent purpose of the organization. If the purpose is sufficiently lofty, this identification infuses their work with meaning, meaning beyond just making a living. Hitting your profit targets each quarter probably isn't much of a transcendent purpose.

Without a transcendent purpose understood and enunciated from on high, the company's direction is at the mercy of the winds of corporate fad and fancy. Shall we become a conglomerate tomorrow?

If all this seems a bit mystical for your taste, try thinking of it in terms of that concept much in vogue nowadays, corporate culture. What, at bottom, is a corporate culture but a set of shared values, values that get reflected in behavior and, in the best cases, further everyone's pursuit of a common end? Each of the well-managed companies listed in *In Search of Excellence*, it should be noted, has a strong culture.

In interviews, authors Peters and Waterman observe that in most cases the culture seemed to be the creation of a strong leader who hammered away at a message to his organization for years. He might be someone who started the company, or who was present almost from the beginning—Tom Watson at IBM—or, considerably less often, someone who rose through the ranks to get the top job, from which bully pulpit he instilled the gospel in a previously less than excellent company—Rene McPherson at Dana. It's enough to make you slightly suspicious of those consultants who offer to help you build a strong corporate culture around your current wimpy management.

The leader's strong ego ideal, coupled with an active but not hyper-critical conscience, has other effects on how he gets along with peers and subordinates. Because his aggressive energies are channeled into the pursuit of a goal larger than himself, when Joe the plant manager lashes out against him in a rage, he won't retaliate in kind. Indeed, if he's the McCoy, he'll probably find some way to help Joe direct his megatonnage against the common task.

The Freudian's typical manager, by comparison, has a conscience that's always keeping score and just maybe poisoning the wellsprings of self-confidence with guilt. All het up with nowhere to go—no very bright ideal to pursue—his aggressive energies will be sluiced into attacks on himself and those around him: he'll distrust his own competence and theirs. The result is corporate politics at its least productive: turf battles, a boss rivalrous toward subordinates and unwilling to help them along, demoralization in all its senses. While the leader devotes himself to getting the job done, the manager worries about "how am *I* doing"—he is a careerist.

The Freudians, as you may imagine, tend to think that the way that we get along with our boss has much to do with how we fared with Mama and Dada. We bring to our dealings with the guy in the corner office feelings of dependency and a need for affection. You scoff: *Affection and dependency—we don't allow those at my company.* No, in the corporate world it's known as seeking recognition, feedback, support. Members of the baby-boom generation, perhaps because they've had to compete to be singled out from their too-numerous peers for so long, are becoming famous for demanding this warm stuff quite explicitly.

The leader—secure, serene in his commitment to task, and looking for people to help him accomplish it——does a better job handling these demands than your average manager. Which, with the accession of baby-boomers to more and more managerial jobs these days, may in part account for why companies seem suddenly to be seeking leader types to yoke the boomers' energies to a corporate purpose. He doesn't just tolerate, he actively encourages all those would-be entrepreneurs in the company skunkworks.

Not that this fabled leader is any kind of cupcake. Because of his overriding commitment to the common goal, and because he's less hung up about his own aggressiveness and others', he can be utterly forthright in telling people when they're not performing up to the mark. If all else has been tried, he can even fire them with a clearer conscience than is common among bureaucrats. Such forthrightness does, however, present special problems for women who would be leaders. Because subordinates expect deep down that the woman who happens to be their boss will be, if anything, more supportive and affectionate than a male—more like Mom—and because women build some of these same expectations into what they demand of themselves, it may be two generations before many women can act as freely, as unconstrainedly, in a leadership role as a man might, at least in Harry Levinson's view.

There are, of course, other problems with this model of a leader, beginning with the question whether any of these paragons actually exist out there in the world. The Freudians are distinctly reluctant to cite examples on the current corporate scene—who knows what his early childhood was like, and whether he really fits the model? Moreover, can the typical large company, with its entrenched bureaucracy, accommodate such a wild man? Probably only if the pain—the pressure from foreign competitors, the inability to overcome economic stagnation—is great enough.

Even if a company were positively hungry for one of these men on horseback, it isn't clear where it would find him. Can leaders be trained, can some latent potential for acting in accordance with the leader's particular psychological makeup be brought out in, say, the average MBA candidate? "We don't know," confesses Harold J. Leavitt, a professor of organizational behavior at Stanford. "We never can tell until we try." Harvard's Zaleznik warns that any attempt to identify potential leaders early in their education and give them special training will have to withstand charges of that most un-American of sins, elitism.

But then, we may not have that much choice if we're going to compete globally with societies that seem to do a better job of fostering and giving rein to leaders. If the prospect gives you pause—and it should—you might want to dwell on the thought that the first endowed chair of leadership in this country bears the name of one Konosuke Matsushita, a peasant's son who in his lifetime managed to build the 33rd-largest industrial corporation in the world.

2
THE ANTILEADERSHIP VACCINE

John W. Gardner

It is generally believed that we need enlightened and responsible leaders—at every level and in every phase of our national life. Everyone says so. But the nature of leadership in our society is very imperfectly understood, and many of the public statements about it are utter nonsense.

This is unfortunate because there are serious issues of leadership facing this society, and we had better understand them.

The Dispersion of Power

The most fundamental thing to be said about leadership in the United States is also the most obvious. We have gone as far as any known society in creating a leadership system that is *not* based on caste or class, nor even on wealth. There is not yet equal access to leadership (witness the remaining barriers facing women and Negroes), but we have come a long, long way from the family—or class-based leadership group. Even with its present defects, ours is a relatively open system.

The next important thing to be said is that leadership is dispersed among a great many groups in our society. The President, of course, has a unique, and uniquely important, leadership role, but beneath him, fragmentation is the rule. This idea is directly at odds with the notion that the society is run by a coherent power group—the Power Elite, as C. Wright Mills called it, or the Establishment, as later writers have named it. It is hard not to believe that such a group exists. Foreigners find it particularly difficult to believe in the reality of the fluid, scattered, shifting leadership that is visible to the naked eye. The real lead-

Reprinted by permission from the 1965 Annual Report, Carnegie Corporation of New York, 437 Madison Avenue, New York 10022.

ership, they imagine, must be behind the scenes. But at a national level this simply isn't so.

In many local communities and even in some states there *is* a coherent power group, sometimes behind the scenes, sometimes out in the open. In communities where such an "establishment," that is, a coherent ruling group, exists, the leading citizen can be thought of as having power in a generalized sense: he can bring about a change in zoning ordinances, influence the location of a new factory, and determine whether the local museum will buy contemporary paintings. But in the dispersed and fragmented power system that prevails in the nation as a whole one cannot say "So-and-so is powerful," without further elaboration. Those who know how our system works always want to know, "Powerful in what way? Powerful to accomplish what?" We have leaders in business and leaders in government, military leaders and educational leaders, leaders in labor and in agriculture, leaders in science, in the world of art, and in many other special fields. As a rule, leaders in any one of these fields do not recognize the authority of leaders from a neighboring field. Often they don't even know one another, nor do they particularly want to. Mutual suspicion is just about as common as mutual respect—and a lot more common than mutual cooperation in manipulating society's levers.

Most of the significant issues in our society are settled by a balancing of forces. A lot of people and groups are involved and the most powerful do not always win. Sometimes a coalition of the less powerful wins. Sometimes an individual of very limited power gets himself into the position of casting the deciding ballot.

Not only are there apt to be many groups involved in any critical issue, but their relative strength varies with each issue that comes up. A group that is powerful today may not be powerful next year. A group that can cast a decisive vote on question A may not even be listened to when question B comes up.

The Nature of Leadership

People who have never exercised power have all kinds of curious ideas about it. The popular notion of top leadership is a fantasy of capricious power: the top man presses a button and something remarkable happens; he gives an order as the whim strikes him, and it is obeyed.

Actually, the capricious use of power is relatively rare except in some large dictatorships and some small family firms. Most leaders are hedged around by constraints—tradition, constitutional limitations, the realities of the external situation, rights and privileges of followers, the requirements of teamwork, and most of all the inexorable demands of large-scale organization, which does not operate on capriciousness. In short, most power is wielded circumspectly.

There are many different ways of leading, many kinds of leaders. Consider for example, the marked contrasts between the politician and the intellectual leader, the large-scale manager and the spiritual leader. One sees solemn descriptions of the qualities needed for leadership without any reference at all to the fact that the necessary attributes depend on the kind of leadership under discussion. Even in a single field there may be different kinds of leadership with different required attributes. Think of the difference between the military hero and the military manager.

If social action is to occur, certain functions must be performed. The problems facing the group or organization must be clarified, and ideas necessary to their solution formulated. Objectives must be defined. There must be widespread awareness of those objectives, and the will to achieve them. Often those on whom action depends must develop new attitudes and habits. Social machinery must be set in motion. The consequences of social effort must be evaluated and criticized, and new goals set.

A particular leader may contribute at only one point to this process. He may be gifted in analysis of the problem, but limited in his capacity to communicate. He may be superb in communicating, but incapable of managing. He may, in short, be an outstanding leader without being good at every aspect of leadership.

If anything significant is to be accomplished, leaders must understand the social institutions and processes through which action is carried out. And in a society as complex as ours, that is no mean achievement. A leader, whether corporation president, university dean, or labor official, knows his organization, understands what makes it move, comprehends its limitations. Every social system or institution has a logic and dynamic of its own that cannot be ignored.

We have all seen men with lots of bright ideas but no patience with the machinery by which ideas are translated into action. As a rule, the machinery defeats them. It is a pity, because the professional and academic man can play a useful role in practical affairs. But too often he is a dilettante. He dips in here or there; he gives bits of advice on a dozen fronts; he never gets his hands dirty working with one piece of the social machinery until he knows it well. He will not take the time to understand the social institutions and processes by which change is accomplished.

Although our decentralized system of leadership has served us well, we must not be so complacent as to imagine that it has no weaknesses, that it faces no new challenges, or that we have nothing to learn. There are grave questions to be answered concerning the leadership of our society. Are we living up to standards of leadership that we have achieved in our own past? Do the conditions of modern life introduce new complications into the task of leadership? Are we failing to prepare leaders for tomorrow?

Here are some of our salient difficulties.

Failure to Cope with the Big Questions

Nothing should be allowed to impair the effectiveness and independence of our specialized leadership groups. But such fragmented leadership does create certain problems. One of them is that it isn't anybody's business to think about the big questions that cut across specialties—the largest questions facing our society. Where are we headed? Where do we *want* to head? What are the major trends determining our future? Should we do anything about them? Our fragmented leadership fails to deal effectively with these transcendent questions.

Very few of our most prominent people take a really large view of the leadership assignment. Most of them are simply tending the machinery of that part of society to which they belong. The machinery may be a great corporation or a great government agency or a great law practice or a great university. These people may tend it very well indeed, but they are not pursuing a vision of what the total society needs. They have not developed a strategy as to how it can be achieved, and they are not moving to accomplish it.

One does not blame them, of course. They do not see themselves as leaders of the society at large, and they have plenty to do handling their own specialized role.

Yet it is doubtful that we can any longer afford such widespread inattention to the largest questions facing us. We achieved greatness in an era when changes came more slowly than now. The problems facing the society took shape at a stately pace. We could afford to be slow in recognizing them, slow in coping with them. Today, problems of enormous import hit us swiftly. Great social changes emerge with frightening speed. We can no longer afford to respond in a leisurely fashion.

Our inability to cope with the largest questions tends to weaken the private sector. Any question that cannot be dealt with by one of the special leadership groups—that is, any question that cuts across special fields—tends to end up being dealt with by government. Most Americans value the role played by nongovernmental leadership in this country and would wish it to continue. In my judgment it will not continue under the present conditions.

The cure is not to work against the fragmentation of leadership, which is a vital element in our pluralism, but to create better channels of communication among significant leadership groups, especially in connection with the great issues that transcend any particular group.

Failure of Confidence

Another of the maladies of leadership today is a failure of confidence. Anyone who accomplishes anything of significance has more confidence than the facts would justify. It is something that outstanding executives have in common with gifted military commanders, brilliant political leaders, and great artists. It is true of societies as well as of individuals. Every great civilization has been characterized by confidence in itself.

Lacking such confidence, too many leaders add ingenious new twists to the modern art which I call "How to reach a decision without really deciding." They require that the question be put through a series of clearances within the organization and let the clearance process settle it. Or take a public opinion poll and let the poll settle it. Or devise elaborate statistical systems, cost-accounting systems, information-processing systems, hoping that out of them will come unassailable support for one course of action rather than another.

This is not to say that leadership cannot profit enormously from good information. If the modern leader doesn't know the facts he is in grave trouble, but rarely do the facts provide unqualified guidance. After the facts are in, the leader must in some measure emulate the little girl who told the teacher she was going to draw a picture of God. The teacher said, "But, Mary, no one knows what God looks like"; and Mary said, "They will when I get through."

The confidence required of leaders poses a delicate problem for a free society. We don't want to be led by Men of Destiny who think they know all the answers. Neither do we wish to be led by Nervous Nellies. It is a matter of balance. We are no longer in much danger, in this society, from Men of Destiny. But we *are* in danger of falling under the leadership of men who lack the confidence to lead. And we are in danger of destroying the effectiveness of those who have a natural gift for leadership.

Of all our deficiencies with respect to leadership, one of the gravest is that we are not doing what we should to encourage potential leaders. In the late eighteenth century we produced out of a small population a truly extraordinary group of leaders—Washington, Adams, Jefferson, Franklin, Madison, Monroe, and others. Why is it so difficult today, out of a vastly greater population, to produce men of that caliber? It is a question that most reflective people ask themselves sooner or later. There is no reason to doubt that the human material is still there, but there is excellent reason to believe that we are failing to develop it—or that we are diverting it into nonleadership activities.

The Antileadership Vaccine

Indeed, it is my belief that we are immunizing a high proportion of our most gifted young people against any tendencies to leadership. It will be worth our time to examine how the antileadership vaccine is administered.

The process is initiated by the society itself. The conditions of life in a modern, complex society are not conducive to the emergence of leaders. The young person today is acutely aware of the fact that he is an anonymous member of a mass society, an individual lost among millions of others. The processes by which leadership is exercised are not visible to him, and he is bound to believe that they are exceedingly intricate. Very little in his experience encourages him to think that he might some day exercise a role of leadership.

This unfocused discouragement is of little consequence compared with the expert dissuasion the young person will encounter if he is sufficiently bright to attend a college or university. In those institutions today, the best students are carefully schooled to avoid leadership responsibilities.

Most of our intellectually gifted young people go from college directly into graduate school or into one of the older and more prestigious professional schools. There they are introduced to—or, more correctly, powerfully indoctrinated in—a set of attitudes appropriate to scholars, scientists, and professional men. This is all to the good. The students learn to identify themselves strongly with their calling and its ideals. They acquire a conception of what a good scholar, scientist, or professional man is like.

As things stand now, however, that conception leaves little room for leadership in the normal sense; the only kind of leadership encouraged is that which follows from the performing of purely professional tasks in a superior manner. Entry into what most of us would regard as the leadership roles in the society at large is discouraged.

In the early stages of a career, there is a good reason for this: becoming a first-class scholar, scientist, or professional requires single-minded dedication. Unfortunately, by the time the individual is sufficiently far along in his career to afford a broadening of interests, he often finds himself irrevocably set in a narrow mold.

The antileadership vaccine has other more subtle and powerful ingredients. The image of the corporation president, politician, or college president that is current among most intellectuals and professionals today has some decidedly unattractive features. It is said that such men compromise their convictions almost daily, if not hourly. It is said that they have tasted the corrupting experience of power. They must be status seekers, the argument goes, or they would not be where they are.

Needless to say, the student picks up such attitudes. It is not that professors propound these views and students learn them. Rather, they are in the air and students absorb them. The resulting unfavorable image contrasts dramatically with the image these young people are given of the professional who is almost by definition dedicated to his field, pure in his motives, and unencumbered by worldly ambition.

My own extensive acquaintance with scholars and professionals on the one hand and administrators and managers on the other does not confirm this contrast in character. In my experience, each category has its share of opportunists. Nevertheless, the negative attitudes persist.

As a result the academic world appears to be approaching a point at which everyone will want to educate the technical expert who advises the leader, or the intellectual who stands off and criticizes the leader, but no one will want to educate the leader himself.

Are Leaders Necessary?

For a good many academic and other professional people, negative attitudes toward leadership go deeper than skepticism concerning the leader's integrity. Many have real doubts, not always explicitly formulated, about the necessity for leadership.

The doubts are of two kinds. First, many scientific and professional people are accustomed to the kinds of problems that can be solved by expert technical advice or action. It is easy for them to imagine that any social enterprise could be managed in the same way. They envisage a world that does not need leaders, only experts. The notion is based, of course, upon a false conception of the leader's function. The supplying of technically correct solutions is the least of his responsibilities.

There is another kind of question that some academic or professional people raise concerning leadership: Is the very notion of leadership somehow at odds with the ideals of a free society? Is it a throwback to earlier notions of social organization?

These are not foolish questions. We have in fact outgrown or rejected several varieties of leadership that have loomed large in the history of mankind. We do not want autocratic leaders who treat us like inferior beings. We do not want leaders, no matter how wise or kind, who treat us like children.

But at the same time that we were rejecting those forms of leadership, we were evolving forms more suitable to our values. As a result our best leaders today are *not* out of place in a free society—on the contrary, they strengthen our free society.

We can have the kinds of leaders we want, but we cannot choose to do without them. It is in the nature of social organization that we must have them at all levels of our national life, in and out of government—in business, labor, politics, education, science, the arts, and every other field. Since we must have them, it helps considerably if they are gifted in the performance of their appointed task. The sad truth is that a great many of our organizations are badly managed or badly led. And because of that, people within those organizations are frustrated when they need not be frustrated. They are not helped when they could be helped. They are not given the opportunities to fulfill themselves that are clearly possible.

In the minds of some, leadership is associated with goals that are distasteful—power, profit, efficiency, and the like. But leadership, properly conceived, also serves the individual human goals that our society values so highly, and we shall not achieve those goals without it.

Leaders worthy of the name, whether they are university presidents or senators, corporation executives or newspaper editors, school superintendents or governors, contribute to the continuing definition and articulation of the most cherished values of our society. They offer, in short, moral leadership.

So much of our energy has been devoted to tending the machinery of our complex society that we have neglected this element in leadership. I am using the word "moral" to refer to the shared values that must undergird any functioning society. The thing that makes a number of individuals a society rather than a population or a crowd is the presence of shared attitudes, habits and values, a shared conception of the enterprise of which they are all a part, shared views of why it is worthwhile for the enterprise to continue and to flourish. Leaders can help in bringing that about. In fact, it is required that they do so. When leaders lose their credibility or their moral authority, then the society begins to disintegrate.

Leaders have a significant role in creating the state of mind that is the society. They can serve as symbols of the moral unity of the society. They can express the values that hold the society together. Most important, they can conceive and articulate goals that lift people out of their petty preoccupations, carry them above the conflicts that tear a society apart, and unite them in the pursuit of objectives worthy of their best efforts.

3
HOW DO LEADERS GET TO LEAD?

Michael M. Lombardo

The question of whether leaders are born or made has vexed organizations throughout history. Even though about 75 percent of management development directors say real development occurs on the job, there is evidence that most organizations allow this development to occur for only a chosen few.

If having the skills and capabilities to become a leader is not as important as the opportunity to develop and demonstrate them, then many managers never have a chance.

The Early Years

A young man might go into military flight training believing that he was entering some sort of technical school in which he was simply going to acquire a certain set of skills. Instead, he found himself all at once enclosed in a fraternity. And in this fraternity, even though it was military, men were not rated by their outward rank as ensigns, lieutenants, commanders, or whatever. "The world was divided into those who had it and those who did not." This quality, this "it," was never named, however, nor was it talked about in any way.

—Tom Wolfe, *The Right Stuff*

Organizations usually separate those who have "it" from those who do not during the early years of a career, and in so doing organizations favor as their future leaders young managers who demonstrate skills and abilities they bring with them to the job. Abilities to work with others, handle conflict, analyze problems, run a meeting, set priorities and so forth are looked for early, and, if seen, can lead to anointment as a high-potential or fast-track manager. If the manager has the right back-

Reprinted by permission from *Issues and Observations*, 2:1 (February 1982), pp. 1–4.

ground as well (e.g., an MBA and past positions of leadership), the odds of being dubbed a rising star increase further.

Organizations put confidence in this rite of anointment to reduce risk. The question of future leadership is a matter of survival. With the vicissitudes of competition, regulation, and the economy, businesses can't afford added uncertainty in the promotion of leaders.

To insure a steady stream of competent leaders, organizations therefore select and hone managers who demonstrate certain skills early. Since learning a management job takes about two years and learning a business takes several decades, organizations take the least risk possible. Although young managers cannot quickly understand the business, they can quickly demonstrate the skills necessary to learn it.

In short, it's easier to teach the objective components of business than it is to teach murky clusters of behavior called skills, or even more difficult to teach abstractions like judgment.

There is more than logic to support the selection of future leaders from among the managers who demonstrate leadership skills early. In Bray and Howard's 20-year study of AT&T managers, there was a shocking finding: The average manager does not improve in managerial abilities over time. There is no evidence that managerial experience is a good teacher of management.

Critics can say that this finding holds for average managers but that those who get to the top are anything but average. Or they might attack the assessment center data on which the Bray and Howard findings are based, contending that the skills and abilities measured are too global to pick up the subtle learning and the refinement of skills that take place over 20 years. A manager who excelled in defining problems 20 years ago may have since developed subtle questioning techniques and ways of turning a problem inside out that a straightforward rating of "clearly defined the problem" might miss.

Still, there is the nagging suspicion that managers who have the skills to begin with have an edge that time only increases. Although most managers in the study indeed changed, becoming both more occupationally and family-oriented, less dependent on others, and more interested in achievement and influencing others, their skills didn't change much. Even for successful managers, interest in personal development and interpersonal skills tended to sag, but (and this is the source of the suspicion) their skills started higher and stayed higher than did the skills of those who were less successful.

It may be that even eventual leaders don't learn many new skills from experience. Instead, they bring their skills to the job, and, as some executives have insisted, rise to the top because their capabilities blossom when they are confronted with new situations. With this view, a manager who jumps in and handles a nasty conflict does so because the requisite skills are waiting within until they are needed.

The Self-Fulfilling Prophevy

If success as a leader were as simple as having the right skills and seizing opportunities to demonstrate them, this view of leadership development could be compelling. But even more important than having the right skills is having the right jobs. Once noticed, fast-movers get into, or are placed in, challenging jobs where they spend more time on projects involving top management, and work for managers who are themselves moving up.

This combination of access to the counsel of top management, working for a highly-regarded manager, and having a core job gives fast-movers the four edges that matter most:

- They learn the business more quickly.
- They learn the perspective of top managers on the business.
- They learn which kinds of jobs and experiences compose the core of the business.
- They more often have a highly-placed mentor to nudge and guide them.

As a result of being seen and being good, the highly-regarded move fast. Leaving their first position in less than two years (according to Veiga), they broaden their perspective with cross-divisional experiences and become expert in one segment of corporate operations.

While not as obvious as being knighted, there is apparently a self-fulfilling prophecy generated whereby success breeds success. By the third year or almost always by the third level of management, potential leaders have been spotted and from then on are exposed to jobs that provide experience relevant for higher-level jobs.

These experiences create expanding opportunities for high-potential managers to learn things far beyond management skills. One group of successful executives, reflecting on the significant learnings in their careers, came up with the following list:

- *Learning to delegate.* Many managers do it all until they pass middle-management, rarely delegating or keeping subordinates adequately informed. Once they become executives, however a change in outlook must be made: Rather than enjoying doing something, executives must enjoy seeing it done. There must be a letting go of hands-on control in favor of in-out advice.

- *Learning how to get advice.* Many managers excel at aggressively seeking information and taking charge. Executives must learn how to communicate the need for advice and information, and how to listen to others' concerns.
- *Setting life goals.* Although managers may conduct their lives by just letting things happen, executives must learn to make career and life decisions based on specific, incremental goals.
- *Discovering strengths.* To take advantage of the opportunities that come to them, executives must learn what it is they are good at doing.
- *Dealing with adversity.* Executives must learn not to over-analyze the past when they are confronted with a failure. They must quickly understand what went wrong, accept responsibility for their part in the failure, and then move on.
- *Struggling with change.* Executives must learn how to take on new and demanding roles, to deal with a changing organization, new technology, and changing societal norms.

Managers not seen by their organizations as fast-trackers face a different experience. They leave their first position later (3-4 years), and often work in peripheral units for so-so managers. Although they, too, change jobs often, the pattern of their moves is less coherent.

They often switch across functional lines, garnering assignments that hinder the development of long-term business contacts (their network) and make it difficult to master any one segment of the business. (The opportunity to learn marketing or manufacturing or legal affairs in detail is critical to later success. In one study, presidents and board chairmen spent as much as two-thirds of their careers in the same function.)

The experiences that non-fast-trackers are exposed to are more narrow and specific. They learn how to implement decisions, set procedures, and master the technical side of management systems, but rarely do they have the opportunity to learn or practice the kinds of skills mentioned by more successful managers.

Haves and Have Nots

A man either had it or he didn't! There was no such thing as having most of it.

—Tom Wolfe, *The Right Stuff*

Whether by nature or by nurture or by both, by about the third level of management, groups of "haves" and "have nots" form in many organizations. For the "haves," their past opportunities have helped them to develop patterns of behavior that are seen as effective in their present jobs and they remain eligible for the top.

For the "have nots"—those who lacked some of the skills to begin with—their problems have been compounded by dead-end, low-visibility jobs which further hinder the catching up they need to do. Real differences now exist between the groups, differences that were there to begin with and that have been exacerbated by later experiences. (See Figure 3.1.)

For the "have nots," a self-defeating pattern emerges: They only listen long enough to categorize a problem then they shoot from the hip with a standardized solution. If the problem reappears, thornier than ever, they waffle and shunt it off to a committee or they go to the other extreme and attempt to overwhelm the problem with a barrage of solutions. At no time do they stop and ask the questions that might tell them what the problem really is.

For the "haves," the essential difference is an ability to break set, to go against the grain of habit. Many managers who become successful embody an oppositeness of nature that enables them to pause long enough to listen to the music of organizational problems, heads craned for that one funny note, then, once they understand what's going on, to act quickly to hammer out the lyrics.

The Right Stuff?

> . . . the idea was to prove at every foot of the way up that pyramid that you were one of the elected and anointed ones who had "the right stuff" and could move higher and higher and even—ultimately, God willing, one day—that you might be able to join that special few at the very top, that elite who had the capacity to bring tears to men's eyes, the very Brotherhood of the Right Stuff itself.
>
> —Tom Wolfe, *The Right Stuff*

Such divergent patterns beg the question of "Are these groups really different or did they grow to be this way?" Or more simply, "Is there such a thing as the right stuff?"

There may well be. The problem is no one knows what the right stuff is, since it is the result of both the nature and the nurture of managers.

Most administrative and interpersonal skills are learnable, so these cannot form any unique set of talents. Conceptual abilities, however,

Fig. 3.1. The Haves and the Have Nots

HAVE NOTS	HAVES
Creatures of habit; tend to wing it based on what worked previously; management by cliche ("never firefight;" "the key to management is delegation")	Analyze each situation; may appear inconsistent because seemingly similar situations in fact aren't
Consistently err at the extremes of behavior— they may never get into detail, or may become obsessed with all details	May get into fine detail on one problem and totally ignore detail on the next; act according to the nature of the problem, not the nature of their habits
Work on whatever comes up (12 problems at once in one study)	Spend a third to a half of their time working on one or two priorities
Lack boldness; hesitate to make decisions on complex problems	Involve lots of people, listen to different views of the problem, play with ideas; once mind is made up, act quickly
Don't seek enough advice or help (limited network of contacts)	Extensive network of contacts who might be located anywhere inside or outside the organization
Personal and work-related blind spots resulting from inadequate feedback (e.g., believe they are superb delegators while their subordinates believe the opposite)	Job interests are balanced with family, friends, and other interests that provide helpful feedback

are developed fairly early in life and although they can be modified a little, no one has as yet figured out how to improve them dramatically.

Teaching good judgment, or the ability to break set, or the ability to pick key problems, or the courage to make unpopular decisions is not something that can be reduced to simple formulas. Such abilities are terribly complex, and require dealing with ambiguity as a matter of course.

If there is such a thing as the right stuff, it probably lies in a certain comfort with the unknown, and in the ability to make sense of the discordant notes that most of us never even hear. But even if we assume that such an ineffable quality exists, many managers never get much opportunity to show it. Perhaps more important, they may never have had the life experiences that create the credentials that make them visible.

So What?

The point is this: By creating opportunities for more young managers and by avoiding premature decisions on managerial careers, organizations can increase their chances of developing the best possible leaders for the future.

For a host of reasons, many managers who may have the right stuff will not have the background experiences and skills that will enable them to show it. Blacks, women, and "late-bloomers" are frequently mentioned as three talent pools who may have had inadequate opportunities to develop.

Here are some suggestions for ways to create opportunities for managers.

- Have a committee of executives address the question, "What should our leaders look like 20 years from now?" (Otherwise, organizations run the risk of promoting only those managers who fit the model of leadership in use 20 years ago.) Decide what developmental experiences the leaders of the year 2000 could benefit from.
- Besides the traditional emphasis on skills and business training for young managers, conduct symposia on the significant events and major learnings of successful executives. These symposia should be small, informal, and conducted by the executives themselves.
- Many organizations have coaching and counseling programs for managers. Organizations could benefit from an executive mentoring program as well. Assign each management recruit to a mentor who meets with the recruit at least once a month for lunch. Ask the mentor to advise the recruit on the recruit's most pressing problems, at the same time injecting top management's perspective into the discussions. Besides getting advice, recruits may be able to learn the business more quickly and understand how successful managers attack problems.
- Give young managers who have lightly-regarded bosses a chance to work with an effective role model at least part of the time.
- Before deciding that some managers don't have it, answer the question, "Have they ever been in a position where they could show it?"

None of these suggestions will produce miracles. Nor will they create wheat from chaff. They may, however, produce some pleasant surprises.

PART 2
THE CORE
INGREDIENTS

Central to leadership are power and influence; they are implicit as well as explicit in the process of leading. At the same time, there are the more subtle notions of intuition and visioning. If a leader is to help define the future, he or she must assist in creating a vision, articulate it (give it meaning), and transform it into action. How that is done is not precise. We know, however, that directions and decisions are sometimes more intuitive than rational. Thus, the ingredients for leadership include the practical applications of power and influence with the general feelings of what to do—intuition and visioning.

Power and Influence

Many people express a discomfort with the idea of power. Yet, leaders must be comfortable with the use of power and realize its limitations. All too often people will see leadership only as an influence process, avoiding the reality that there is also a power dimension. Neither power nor influence is inherently good or bad. Both are necessary for successful leadership. It is the "how" or the process that has a value dimension.

We can view power as the ability to control resources. This control can be well defined as budget or decision authority. Power is the ability to make things happen; we can give resources or we can take them away. As we move into a knowledge-based society, access to information has become a strong base of power. Thus, the leader is charged with identifying the sources of power, acquiring the necessary resources, and using them in a way that allows people in organizations to achieve their objectives. Because many examples relate to the misuse of power, we are hesitant to talk about acquiring power bases. The truth is, no one can do anything without people, money, materials, information, and time. Leaders are responsible for ensuring that those resources are available when needed.

But the leader does not have to horde the resources. In fact, collaborative leadership is less dependent simply on a source of power than it is on empowering the group to acquire the needed resources. Empowerment is really a sharing; giving others the ability to use the resources in the best way so that the goals are achieved. Leaders do not have to retain the control. Rather, leadership involves assisting everyone working with the organization to collectively gain control over the resources for the common good. It is getting something done through others; the leader removes the obstacles. Empowerment is a broader concept than the traditional notion of power.

Influence may be viewed as a form of power, one of ideas and beliefs. We can get people to respond by using power—the giving or withholding of specific resources. We can also have people respond because they want to; they believe in our ideas or share in our commitment. This is influence. We separate the concepts when power involves resources and influence is a function of personalities.

What is important is the ownership of ideas and action. This can occur either through empowerment or influence. The impact is to create an environment for leadership that involves the commitment of everyone. There are many people identifying a broader range of resources, and they share a common understanding. Further, everyone accepts how resources are used. Finding the right combination of power and influence depends on the self confidence of the leader (can I *really* share this?) and the willingness of others to accept responsibility (do we want to be held accountable for the results?).

Charting the Course

Nearly every definition of leadership includes vision. What distinguishes leaders from others is that they can "see" a future state of affairs for the organization. Their belief or passion for achieving that end is the driving force for their leadership. Often, this vision is not clearly understood by others and it is not a logical extension of the present. Leaders must make it understood if they are to empower others.

The leader is the storyteller. Through the use of language and symbols, the vision of the future is captured in a phrase or a logo. Leadership is distilling a complex future event in a precise way so that everyone inside and outside the organization can understand it. Language is the least visible component but the most influential; it gives vision a shared meaning that comes from shared experiences. At every occasion, the leader tells the story so that the vision is felt—it is believed.

Vision creates a focus of what is possible; it is almost mystical. It starts out as a dream intended for reality. A dream invests small words with deep meaning. Then, there can be a cocreation of the vision. As the story develops, everyone gets to contribute. Soon, there is a feeling that we all have "a piece of the action." Over time, the vision becomes clearer. As each person in the organization has a chance to write the story, the future is cocreated and reality seems possible. The leader must continue to tell the story in a variety of ways to give the vision meaning, developing and maintaining the confidence of organization members.

As we move from the present to the future, action decisions must be made. There are an infinite number of management tools and computer models to give us optimal decision alternatives. Managers define the boundaries and constraints to allow room for creative and innovative decisions. Leaders process that same information and add a new dimension—intuition. Gut feelings are important and effective leaders develop a great confidence in doing what "feels" good. (But, there are seldom "long shots," "high flyers," or "crap shoots.")

Intuition is using information we have learned but using it in different ways and combinations that do not appear inherently logical. If we simply extrapolated the past, charting the course would be relatively easy. When we allow our intuition to flow freely, bold constructions of things that we know emerge. The result is creativity and vision.

Application of our creative processes is most often associated with entrepreneurship. New visions and new ideas spawn the products and services of tomorrow. This is a form of leadership necessary to new as well as existing organizations. In many respects, we can see the entrepreneur as a leader, for leaders are certainly risk takers.

Leadership

Leaders must develop a confidence in understanding and using the core ingredients. There is a certain comfort level with power just as there is with intuition. The essence of these ingredients is a sense of self-knowledge—knowing who we are and where we are going. There is a fine line in every organizational leadership situation where power can be abused and misused. Creating a vision that is ahead of one's time can cause a person to be viewed as irrational rather than visionary. Entrepreneurs are one step from being just another person with a crazy idea. In this section, we provide perspectives that enable the leader to understand the important differences.

Bartolomé and Laurent take a good look at power in "The Manager: Master and Servant of Power." Their approach is special in that they examine power in terms of how it affects the interpersonal relationships in organizations.

Perhaps the best description of a visionary is in Marshall Sashkin's "The Visionary Leader." He separates the leader with vision from visionary leadership, capturing the concept of cocreation. Most importantly, he provides a framework for turning the vision into reality.

Richard Molz then presents the concept of the entrepreneur as visionary, and he describes the process of innovation. In "Entrepreneurial Managers in Large Organizations," he shows how organizations can nurture creativity, combining intuition with power to address the long term.

Finally, the importance of self-knowledge is highlighted in "High Hurdles: The Challenge of Executive Self-Development," by Robert Kaplan, Wilfred Drath, and Joan Kofodimos. The difference in their approach is that they are looking at people who have made it to the top rather than those who aspire to the top. We selected this article because it examines the need to develop shortcomings. There are interesting approaches to power and "elevation."

There *are* central ingredients to effective leadership. They are not tools or techniques. Rather, they are values and beliefs that the leader develops from within. They create an environment for people to be productive and satisfied in while experiencing personal and professional growth.

4
THE MANAGER: MASTER AND SERVANT OF POWER

Fernando Bartolomé and André Laurent

Most managers are action oriented. As a result, many are not inclined to be introspective about how they relate to others on the job. They don't fully realize, for example, how power differences can disturb interpersonal relations at work and, consequently, undermine organizational effectiveness.

Let's look at three typical problems:

■ Brian Dolan and John Miller, both senior engineers in an electronics company, had worked well as colleagues in their company's R&D department. Their relationship was friendly and informal. Each felt free to drop in unannounced on the other to discuss technical problems or swap company gossip.

Then Brian was promoted to director of R&D, and shortly thereafter he called John and asked him to come to his office to discuss installation plans for the company's new computer-aided design system. The call puzzled and angered John. Brian was only two doors away. Why didn't he just drop by? After all, they were good friends. Why did he have to play the boss? When John went to Brian's office, it was all he could do to hide his irritation. Brian greeted him warmly, but John was reserved during their discussion.

Why, Brian wondered on the trip home that evening, had John acted so oddly? Was it because he had been promoted and not John? That had to be it. John was jealous. John, on the other hand, didn't understand how Brian's new position could make him insensitive to how John might react.

■ Mary Scarpa, divisional director for a specialty steel fabricator, asked Roger Harrison, a middle manager, for his opinion on a major capital investment decision she was about to make. Roger had serious reservations about the assumptions underlying her cash flow projections. He wanted to level with her, but he also worried that honest criticism would upset her. He knew Mary could be very touchy. Although she had asked for candid feedback, Roger wasn't sure she really meant it; he sensed she really wanted reinforcement. Feeling caught in a bind, Roger conveniently "forgot" her request.

Annoyed by Roger's behavior, Mary complained to a colleague at another company about problems with her subordinates, saying they just wouldn't stick their necks out. They were afraid to give honest opinions because they were insecure, she said. On his part, Roger was insensitive to the reasons why bosses may find it risky to have subordinates challenge their judgment, even when they ask for it.

■ Dick Rapp, vice president of production for a household appliance manufacturer, told his subordinates that his priority was quality control and cost containment. He wanted defect and scrap rates brought down. He wanted the division to be results driven, not rule driven. "If you have to bend a rule to get the job done, do it," Rapp would say.

His employees took him at his word at first and assumed that any improvement in efficiency would be welcome. But they quickly learned otherwise. Dick Rapp cared as much about style and form as he did about substance. How memos were worded and typed, for example, seemed to concern him as much as what they said. He also chewed out several plant supervisors for approving ad hoc scheduling and other changes and not going through the chain of command.

Understandably, this behavior frustrated Dick's subordinates. They faced conflicting expectations, and they had to take time away from important tasks to meet what they considered frivolous demands. No one tried to understand, though, why bosses prefer to have things done their way and how this may be their means of heightening their feelings of being in control and reducing uncertainty. And nobody dared to explore these issues with Dick, nor could he see that he was sending mixed messages and burying people in the very red tape he wanted them to cut through.

How did these situations develop? Did Brian Dolan subconsciously need to pull rank on subordinates? Did Mary Scarpa relish putting her employees in a double bind? Did Dick Rapp enjoy tripping up his people? Were the subordinates rebellious people, unwilling to accept authority and take direction? Such problems occur with surprising frequency in work situations. Usually they arise not because superiors are inherently insensitive or power hungry or because subordinates are naturally rebellious but because people don't understand how strongly hierarchical position affects behavior in organizations. Workplace conflicts are often attributed to personality differences, but the root of the problem is usually structural. The organization's power hierarchy can distort mutual expectations.

Power in the Organization

Unevenness of power in the organization subtly influences how managers and subordinates relate to each other. Mary couldn't understand Roger's reticence. But if she had reflected on her own experiences as a subordinate, she might have realized that she too had been cautious at times about giving honest feedback to superiors. Had Brian been able to put himself in John's shoes and think of a new R&D director officiously summoning *him*, he might have better understood John's behavior.

Dick was a results-driven manager who said he cared about quality, not style. Today he works for superiors whose preference for ritualistic, by-the-book action frustrates him. Yet he can't see that he's doing the same thing. He doesn't relate his own experience as a subordinate to the feelings and behavior of the people working for him.

Brian, Mary, and Dick all had trouble putting themselves in their subordinates shoes. In subordinate roles, on the other hand, John and Roger couldn't see how it might feel to be a boss. This lack of sensitivity on both sides can have ripple effects throughout the organization. Managers who believe they are on the receiving end of unreasonable or unfair actions from their bosses, for example, may act similarly toward those below them in the organizational pyramid. And the pattern may repeat itself down the chain of command. Or relations with peers may suffer. A troubled relationship at one level can affect many other relationships.

When superiors can't see how their behavior affects their subordinates, their authority may also deteriorate. Most bosses know instinctively that their power depends more on employees' compliance than on threats or sanctions. When managers create no-win situations for people, as Mary did, or make confusing demands on workers, as did Dick, subordinates may respond by losing enthusiasm or withdrawing commitment. If workers think they've been put in impossible situations or if a superior's exaggerated need for power makes them feel inferior, they may give the company their worst rather than their best. The response could mean just going through the motions of the job or even sabotaging organizational goals.

True, managers have power. They can call on official sanctions for punishing uncooperative subordinates. But such blatant use of their clout is rarely able to restore effective working relationships. It is a weak rather than a strong pillar of authority.

There are other consequences arising from this asymmetry in power relations and role perceptions, as we can see when we look at managers as subordinates. If the danger for superiors is being insufficiently sensitive about their subordinates' potential reactions, the danger for subordinates tends to be excessive concern about superiors' potential reactions. Managers who worry excessively about offending their bosses are much less likely to defend subordinates when higher-ups deal unfairly with them.

But if a manager doesn't defend subordinates, he or she will lose their respect. When subordinates sense that the boss won't defend them against unfairness, their morale will plummet and they will withdraw commitment to the job. A vicious circle results. As their performance deteriorates, their superior's position weakens further. The boss will receive fewer rewards and resources to dispense to subordinates, thus further undermining his or her effectiveness as distinct from merely titular authority.

It's ironic that so many managers are insensitive to this problem because almost all managers occupy a dual position in the organization. They have subordinates who report to them, and they report to superiors. Being both masters and servants of power, they should be able to understand the perspectives of the two groups of people who play the most important roles in their professional lives—namely, their superiors and subordinates.

To probe this duality of the manager's role and the sharp differences in expectations that power differences create, we recently collected questionnaires from 105 executives of major companies. We divided the people into two similar groups, matched according to age, management position, and other characteristics. We asked one group of managers to describe the expectations they had for their superiors, the second to describe expectations for subordinates. In addition, we had conversations with a number of the executives we surveyed.

Fig. 4.1. Comparison of Role Expectations

	Desired traits	Percentage of managers who mentioned this trait Multiple choices were possible
What managers expect from subordinates	Good task performance	78%
	Loyalty and obedience	60
	Honesty	53
	Initiative	31
	Other skills	26
What managers expect from superiors	Good communication and feedback	64%
	Leadership	60
	Encouragement and support	50
	Delegation and autonomy	37
	Professional competence	21
	Information	17

As Figure 4.1 shows, the expectations of the two groups differed sharply. Of the managers we asked to take the superior role, 78% said they are primarily concerned about subordinates' performance. A majority also said they expect subordinates to be loyal and honest. A typical comment was "I expect effective performance and loyalty even when difficult or unpleasant duties have to be performed."

The superiors we talked to view loyalty, honesty, and performance as linked. They also see honest communication and a willingness to follow orders as necessary to get the job done. But at the same time, they don't see the potential conflict that lies in demanding loyalty and desiring honesty and frankness from subordinates. Many seem unaware of the extent to which they confuse loyalty with agreement and obedience. They also seem to underestimate the difficulty subordinates have in being honest about their own problems or weaknesses with people who have so much influence on their careers.

What happens when the shoe is on the other foot?

When managers take the subordinate position, they expect leadership and good communication from their superiors. A director of finance we talked to said, "I expect my superior to give me clear messages about what he expects from me." A vice president of engineering commented, "The boss should establish his requirements absolutely clearly."

Why do subordinates want clear communication and decisive leadership from their superiors? One reason is that they need reassurance that their bosses are competent. Clear communication is a good measure of competence. Subordinates also want to minimize uncertainty in their environment. Clear communication reduces guesswork. But decisiveness and clarity of communication alone aren't enough. Our interviews revealed that subordinates also want consistency.

Managers in both interview groups gave initiative and autonomy much lower ratings than we had expected. Fewer than a third of the people who took the superior role said they expect initiative from subordinates. Only 37% of those in the subordinate position said it is important for their superiors to grant them autonomy. This is odd when one considers how strongly management experts today endorse job autonomy and broad participation in decision making.

Subordinates don't want superiors to be constantly peering over their shoulders. Instead, they want enough leeway to do the jobs as they see fit. "The boss shouldn't interfere in details," a sales manager said, and "My manager should give me enough space to do my job," said an administrative officer.

Subordinates also want fair performance appraisals, support, and encouragement. Another sales manager said, "My superior should show fairness, objectivity, honesty, and a willingness to give feedback without my having to ask for it." A division manager answered, "I expect help, encouragement, and coaching, and the opportunity to learn from my mistakes." And an R&D director reported, "I expect support in conflict situations."

Managers as Superiors

As bosses, managers are not only often unaware of how they misuse their power in relation to subordinates, but they are also frequently unaware of the contradictory messages they send and their motives for doing so. For example, they may tell subordinates that they expect them to be candid and to feel free to offer criticism. Yet at the same time, they communicate disapproval of candid feedback through subtle and sometimes not so subtle cues.

Managers may even confuse excessive deference (pleasing behavior) with the normal level of compliance that they feel they have a legitimate right to expect. They may not see the ways in which they signal to subordinates demands for excessively deferential behavior—and they are also often unaware of the deep resentment that these demands produce.

In the superior role, most managers say that they are more concerned about their subordinates' performance than with obedience for its own sake or with workers doing things the boss's way. Despite the overt message they send, however—"good performance is what really counts in my department"—many managers communicate subtly to subordinates that obedience and deference are just as important, if not more so. This is usually subconscious on the managers' part.

Most executives have trouble learning about the expectations their subordinates have of them simply because they are rarely forthright about how they'd like *their* bosses to behave. Actually, most subordinates work hard to adapt their behavior to what they think the boss expects. Although the chief's actions may be very frustrating to them, few will express openly their dislike of the behavior or try to persuade the boss to change—even when invited to criticize.

This reticence can lead to surprising angry outbursts when smoldering resentment suddenly surfaces. The superior ends up wondering, "Why didn't you come to me earlier with this problem?" Bosses will often deny blame and claim they've always had an open-door policy. Many apparently assume that such a policy alone is sufficient to guarantee a fully open relationship and to minimize the effects of power.

Managers as Subordinates

As subordinates, managers develop an exaggerated concern over pleasing their bosses because they believe they have very little power to change the superior's behavior. Whatever the boss's rhetoric may be, they are convinced they know the real score. As a result, they spend much time scrutinizing the boss's behavior for cues that indicate approval or disapproval.

As one manager put it "I suppose it's true: I study [my manager's] likes, dislikes, and other personal tastes; his objectives and motivations and the time pressure he may be under." One division head said of his superior, "I take into account how his thinking differs from mine, what things he is likely to view in a different way."

Managers as superiors know how much they depend on their subordinates' performance and, therefore, how much real power, as opposed to formal power, their subordinates have over them. But when bosses are subordinates, they often forget this reality of organizational life. They forget that the boss's performance depends heavily on how committed the subordinates are to their jobs and on the quality of their work. Consequently, the subordinates often seem to focus too much on accommodating their superiors' stylistic preferences and not enough on performance per se. They don't always recognize that they possess real power that they can use with their bosses to negotiate and obtain satisfaction for their legitimate needs and demands. They seem unable to transfer their experiences as bosses to their behavior as subordinates.

Because subordinates perceive themselves as being too weak to alter their superiors' behavior, managers in the subordinate role are extremely concerned with whether they have a natural match ("good chemistry") with their bosses. When relating to subordinates, on the other hand, managers don't seem concerned about compatibility. They assume that their subordinates can easily learn to conform to their expectations and that this reshaping of behavior will not harm the organization. In reality, however, having to adapt like this is likely to keep subordinates from making a full contribution. In most cases, inhibiting people this way creates resentment.

Consequences of Power

When managers fail to understand how deeply the unequal distribution of power can hurt interpersonal relations and productivity, serious problems can arise for the organization. The most important and pervasive negative effect of the hierarchical structure can be summarized in the saying, "Trust flees authority." Good ideas often remain unexpressed because subordinates believe they will be punished for disagreeing with their superiors or showing too much competence. Honest feedback about the superior's managerial style is withheld because subordinates are afraid they'll be blackballed when decisions on promotions are made.

Reducing the upward flow of ideas and feedback can have many adverse consequences. Take, for example, the many MBO [management by objectives] programs that run into difficulty. An honest contract between superiors and subordinates, based on a fair exchange of contributions and rewards between the individuals and the organization, should be at the core of an MBO program. This is only possible, however, if subordinates feel that they will not be punished for defending their interests or balking at unreasonable demands from the top. Unfair

MBO agreements may work in the short run, but they will usually fail in the long haul.

When managers are dissatisfied with the contracts they have with their bosses, unfair contracts may follow at each level down the ladder. Such a pattern can damage management's credibility as well as the whole organization's authority.

What Can Managers Do?

Nobody is to blame for these distortions of hierarchical power. The problem is inherent in organizational life because authority differences are both inevitable and also functional to a degree. The problem cannot be avoided, but it can be controlled if managers strive to link their two roles as masters and servants of power.

When they are in the superior role, they should ask themselves, "How would I feel if my boss behaved this way or demanded this of me?" For example, Brian in our first case might have stopped to think, "I need to talk to John, but if I summon him, he may think I'm trying to remind him that I got the promotion and he didn't. And why, after all, am I doing this? Can't I get the information just as well by phone? Come to think of it, I remember the time I got angry when *my* boss asked me to come running on a moment's notice."

Managers can also ask whether the tasks they assign to subordinates are truly critical to the job—as distinct from ritualistic demands motivated by an unconscious desire to show people that "rank has its privileges" or to reassure themselves that they can make people do what they want them to do. "Power: use it or lose it," as another saying goes.

The burden for getting relationships back on a healthy basis falls mainly to bosses because they have more power and because it would be unrealistic to expect subordinates to take the initiative and complain about their bosses' unreasonable or unfair conduct. Even if superiors encourage honest feedback, people rarely believe that they mean it. So, generally they won't risk testing the boss's sincerity.

When they are the superior, managers need to ask themselves, "What can I do to increase my employees' trust, or at least decrease their mistrust? What signals may indicate problems?" Managers need to learn to monitor subordinates' subtle cues. It helps to understand that it's easier for subordinates to learn about bosses reactions and desires because superiors are more likely to express their feelings openly. By the same token, it's more difficult for bosses to find out their subordinates' real feelings; they're likely to express them indirectly and with caution.

Directly questioning subordinates rarely works when you're trying to find out what's wrong. Managers must look for subtle cues. Eventually, they can create the necessary atmosphere of trust for solving problems, but they can't do it instantly. It will come only from consistently demonstrating fairness and honesty toward the people working for them.

In the subordinate role, on the other hand, managers may find that they can more easily manage their relationships with superiors by just asking them what they want. This approach should work with competent and insightful superiors. But for some people, asking questions may not be enough; observing behavior is often equally important. Once again, the managerial subordinate should take advantage of his or her own experience as a boss and ask, "What do I care most about when I'm in the superior role?" Managers who can answer this question insightfully and realistically should be able to move ahead in the important process of understanding and managing their own superiors.

5
THE VISIONARY LEADER

Marshall Sashkin

History has been thought of by some as the story of great leaders. Through the first half of this century, most managers as well as scholars probably accepted the basic premises of the "great person" theory of leadership. It was at about that time that early studies at Harvard showed that only a small proportion of leaders actually fit this stereotype. Subsequent theories of leadership centered on behavior; perhaps if someone were to act like a great leader, the act would become real. It was becoming somewhat clearer just how leaders do behave, so perhaps it was reasonable to train people to act that way.

But the next 30 years of leadership research failed to yield substantial evidence that leaders who behaved in a task-directed manner, while simultaneously behaving in a relationship-directed manner, were especially successful or "great." Thus, researchers turned to situational factors in the hope that different behavioral approaches might be effective in different situations. This approach did not, however, help them understand any better how executive leaders succeed. Researchers were still at a loss for explaining outstanding leadership at the top—leadership characterized by vision.

My theory of effective executive leadership, or visionary leadership, considers not just the leaders, not just the leader's behavior, and not just the situation; it considers all three. Only by looking at each of these factors can we truly understand the visionary leadership exemplified by Lee Iacocca (Chrysler), Tom Watson, Sr. (IBM), Rene McPherson (Dana), and Jack Welch (GE). These individuals share certain characteristics different from the personality traits early leadership research focused on. Plus, these executives all have a deep, basic awareness of key situational factors that dictate what leadership approach and actions

Reprinted by permission from the *Training and Development Journal*, 40:5 (May 1986), pp. 58-61, copyright 1986, Marshall Sashkin.

are required. Furthermore, all these people know what behaviors are required for effective visionary leadership, and all can carry out those behaviors.

Furthermore, all these people know what behaviors are required for effective visionary leadership, and all can carry out those behaviors.

Visionary leadership really means three things. It means that the leader is able to develop long-range visions of what his or her organization can and should become. These visions are usually detailed only in the short range. Still, the leader could, if pressed, fill in step-by-step details from beginning to end, though the end might be 10, 20, or more years in the future. Visionary leadership also means that the leader understands the key elements of a vision, what must be included in a vison if it is to direct the organization into the future. Finally, it means that the leader can communicate his or her visions in ways that are compelling, ways that make people want to buy into the leader's vision and help make it happen.

Visioning

More basic than the key elements of a vision, and more important than getting the vision across, is the ability to create a vision. This ability is not very common, especially in terms of long time spans. It is a rare individual who can think and plan clearly over a 10- or 20-year time span. But, whether one is involved in creating a 10-year or 10-week vision, the ability to do so involves four distinct actions, each requiring certain thinking skills.

The first such skill is in *expressing* the vision—behaving in a way that advances the goal of the vision. Consider the case of a manufacturer's chief executive who wishes to create a plant-level operation to involve all employees in managing the firm. To make this vision real, the CEO must be able to perform these steps:

- write a proposed set of policy actions that would create a plant level worker involvement program
- meet with relevant parties—plant-level managers as well as workers—to develop a document detailing the new policy and program
- meet with, and arrange meetings of, all plant-level managers and all employees to review and revise the program, and to plan for its implementation
- work with relevant managers to identify ways to track the program's effects and effectiveness

■ oversee the monitoring of the program, and work with relevant parties on any further modifications needed.

Expressing, then, calls for the leader to understand and perform the sequence of actions he or she must take to make a vision real.

The second thinking skill necessary is in *explaining* the vision to others—making the nature of the vision clear in terms of its required action steps and its aims. Using again the example of the CEO who envisions worker involvement at the plant level: The CEO who can express this vision still may not succeed in implementing it unless he or she can clearly explain the steps of the vision. Unless the CEO can explain the vision to the program manager, constant uncertainty will arise as to steps and handling of problems and issues. Unless the CEO can explain the program to plant managers, their support for the vision will fade as the CEO loses touch with the day-to-day program details (as is inevitable for any chief executive). Explaining involves more than mere restatement of the vision's nature or aim. The visionary leader must be able to describe how the actions required for the vision link together to attain its goal.

The third required thinking skill is in *extending* the vision—applying the sequence of activities to a variety of situations so that the vision can be implemented in several ways and places. To continue with the above example, the CEO will probably, at some point wish to extend the vision to other parts of the organization. This might mean working with the program manager to revise the worker involvement plan and apply it to the headquarters staff departments, as well as to the plant. Doing so will call for changes in how the program is implemented, and may even require alterations in the worker involvement program itself. The expressed vision is an important frame of reference, but the visionary leader must be able to adapt it to varied circumstances, as required. Again, he or she must be able to explain these changes.

The fourth thinking skill involves *expanding* the vision—applying it not just in one limited way, and not even in a variety of similar ways, but in many different ways in a wide range of circumstances. The CEO who has a vision of worker involvement at the plant level, and who goes about implementing this vision in the manner outlined above, still may not be a visionary leader. The true visionary leader will also have the conceptual skill needed to look at the overall plan and effects of worker involvement in the organization. This means more than extending the program to another unit. The visionary leader will think through the spread of the worker involvement vision throughout the organization, consider different ways the program might be spread (for example, unit by unit, or by divisions), and think about how to "revise" the entire organization to be consistent with the new employee involvement system.

Just about anyone can carry out the four skills of visioning—expressing, explaining, extending, and expanding—with respect to short-range visions—ones implemented in a day, a week, a month, or a year. Few people can do so over periods of one to three years; fewer still can vision over periods of five to ten years. The person who can think through a vision over a time span of 10 to 20 years is the rare, visionary leader.

The Vision

I have identified the process of creating a vision, but have said little about just what a vision is. Is it a consistently prepared hamburger, as in the case of Ray Kroc's vision for McDonald's of a hamburger that would be exactly the same whether served in Tokyo or Tulsa? Is a vision a plumper, healthier, "yellower" chicken, as in the case of Frank Perdue, who created a chicken empire based on the premise that quality has no limits? Is it being "one percent better than the competition" at a thousand little things, the vision of Jan Carlzon, CEO of Scandinavian Airlines System (SAS)?

It is all of these and none of them. Visions vary infinitely in the specifics of their content. Yet, some basic elements must be dealt with by any vision that is to have a substantial impact on an organization.

One of these elements is *change*. In the case of McDonald's, it is the absence of change in hamburgers, combined with a continued search for new products (McRibs, McD.L.T., etc.). For Frank Perdue it is the incremental change of constant quality improvement. For SAS the vision refers to creating an edge over the competition. Dealing with change means taking hold of and using changing market forces to the advantage of the organization.

Another basic element all visions must incorporate is a *goal*. To an outsider it may seem that a standardized hamburger or milk shake is a trivial goal, but you'd better believe it was not trivial to Ray Kroc, nor is it trivial to executives at McDonald's today. Concern for greater SAS passenger satisfaction, in comparison with competitor's passenger satisfaction, may seem common; Carlzon himself said, "That's been everybody's vision since the beginning of time in this industry." The difference, he went on to say, was "we executed." Visionary leaders make goals that may seem trivial to outsiders, but are critical to those inside the organization.

A final element of an effective vision: It centers on *people* both customers and employees. Perhaps it is obvious that only through people can a vision become real, yet some fine visions neglect to provide roles for people—ways to involve them, to give them responsibility, to let them take charge of the vision and make it their own. If the vision remains an idea of the leader——the leader's "property" not "owned" by the organization's members—it cannot succeed. People are committed to creating the innovations needed to increase the quality of Perdue's hens. People at McDonalds' Hamburger U. are driven with the importance of maintaining quality, service, cleanliness, and value. Those goals, and the aim to standardize hamburgers, can only be attained through the commitment of people.

Why are the elements change, goals, and people? Why not some other set of factors or some additional ones? The answer is both theoretical and pragmatic. On a theoretical level, these three elements are taken from the work of American sociologist Talcott Parsons. Based on a sociological analysis of organizations, Parsons argued that four critical functions must be effectively attended to by any organization in order to survive. One has to do with adapting to change in the environment. The second concerns attaining goals that clients or customers want and will pay for. The third function concerns coordinating ongoing activities, that is, integrating the various behavioral actions of the people who operate the organization. Parsons's fourth proposed function is maintaining the pattern of actions, with respect to adapting, attaining goals, and coordinating people's activities. This pattern of actions is maintained through the development of common beliefs and values, or an organizational culture. The shared beliefs and values defining the culture determine how the company adapts to change, what goals the company aims for, how these goals relate to customer wants, how the company deals with its people, and how the people deal with one another to coordinate their work activities. It is these shared beliefs that the visionary leader strives to construct, define, and gain commitment to—beliefs about change, goals, and people.

These three key issues can also be seen in a purely pragmatic, nontheoretical analysis of organizational excellence. In their book, *In Search of Excellence*, Thomas Peters and Robert Waterman defined eight strategies characteristic of high-performing organizations. In a more recent work, Peters condensed these eight strategies into three. The first of the three strategies is a bias toward entrepreneurial action, which relates to the issue of change. The second key strategy is "keep close to the customer." This clearly has to do with goals. The third concerns the overriding importance of people, which is another way of emphasizing the coordination function identified by Parsons.

When the deepest of theoreticians agrees with the most popular of modern pragmatists, one suspects that significant truths have been uncovered.

Making the Vision Real

A vision is expressed and explained through words and actions in three ways. First, a clear and brief statement of the vision, a sort of organizational philosophy, must be made. This is relatively common for Japanese firms, less so (but not unheard of) among American organizations. Such a statement must be so clear that every person in the organization can express it, from the CEO to the janitor. Even so, no matter how clear and straightforward the statement of philosophy—the vision statement—is, it means nothing unless it is coupled with actions.

A critical second step, therefore, is for the organization to put its money where its mouth is. Policies must be developed, and programs must be initiated to carry out the policies. This requires commitment of resources. One organization, for example, determined that its vision involved people working in teams to produce what had been assembly-line products. This was an expensive vision to implement; initial programs required the expenditure of millions of dollars in redesigning the production process. (Ultimately, the vision was justified; increased profits in two years more than made up for the cost investment.)

While a clear vision statement and actions to support the vision are critical, they are not enough to make the vision real. The third and deciding factor concerns the personal actions of the leader. The leader must communicate the vision in a way that reaches out to people, gripping them and making them want to get involved in carrying out that vision. When a leader is especially successful in getting a vision across, he or she is thought of as charismatic. But charisma is not personal magic; it is the result of effective behaviors the leader engages in to communicate his or her vision.

I identified five charismatic behaviors by studying Warren Bennis's characteristics of exceptionally effective CEO's. Bennis interviewed 90 such individuals and came up with a set of personality characteristics that can be seen as charismatic behaviors.

The first behavior consists of focusing others' attention on key issues—helping people grasp, understand, and become committed to the leader's vision. Notice how Iacocca, in his television commercials, focuses your attention on quality. Frank Perdue grabs your attention and focuses it on chicken quality as indicated by color (white versus yellow). This behavior represents the value placed on customer-centered goals.

Another charismatic behavior is communicating effectively. This means listening for understanding, rephrasing to clarify, giving constructive feedback, (being descriptive and not evaluative, being specific and not general), and summarizing when appropriate. These behaviors are easy to describe, but they take tremendous skill to perform.

In a television interview, Henry Kissinger was once asked if Mao Tse-tung actually held conversations with a person alone with him (as Kissinger was on several occasions) or simply lectured, stating his position and pretty much ignoring the other person's views. Kissinger responded that one could *only* have a give-and-take conversation with Mao; Mao absolutely insisted on hearing a person out, in detail, and never spoke as though he was delivering a position statement, at least not in a one-on-one situation. He would show that he had listened and understood what the other person said, then explain his views briefly and clearly. This style of communication fosters the belief in overriding importance of people.

The third charismatic behavior, also centering on the importance of people, concerns one's consistency and trustworthiness. Bennis found that outstanding CEOs exhibited consistent behavior. They did not ever flip-flop on their positions; it was always clear where they stood on issues. People might not agree with the leader, but they could trust him to mean what he said and say what he meant; he would not shift positions with every shift in the political winds. Perhaps one of the most important reasons why so many American voters rejected Jimmy Carter was that he shifted positions constantly while insisting that he could be trusted.

Displaying respect for self and others is the fourth type of charismatic behavior. One must start with self-respect, since one cannot really care about others unless he or she really cares about him- or herself. The visionary executive leader is self-assured, certain of his or her own abilities. This shows up not in an arrogant or superior attitude, but in a simple display of self-confidence. Bennis gave a good example: Dr. Franklin Murphy, former chancellor of UCLA and now chairman of the Times-Mirror Company, has been offered several appointments to President Reagan's cabinet. Murphy has declined repeatedly. He says, "I just don't think I'd be good at that sort of thing." In other words, he is so certain of himself that he is comfortable in turning down opportunities that most people—anyone who felt pressured to prove personal worth—would have a hard time rejecting. And, he had no second thoughts about it. This sense of self-respect, of confidence in one's self and one's abilities, comes across not just in the leader's attitude about himself. It also shows in how he treats others. One of the characteristics of charismatic leaders is that we feel good around them. This is because they boost our sense of self-worth by paying attention to us, by trusting us, by sharing ideas with us, by making it clear how important we are as persons. They tell us how important we are—"I really value your ability to do that, John; we need you"—and they show us through their behaviors, too. This behavior, even more than the preceding two behaviors, focuses on the importance of people.

The last charismatic behavior involves taking calculated risks and making a commitment to risks once they are decided on. Visionary leaders have no energy to spare for covering their butts; all their efforts go toward achieving their goals. Moveover, these leaders build opportunities into their risks for others to buy in, to take the risks with the leaders and share in the effort and the rewards. These leaders motivate by "pulling" us along with them, as Bennis puts it, rather than by trying to push us in the direction they want to go. Franklin D. Roosevelt displayed this sort of behavior often; he took risks and made commitments, and inspired others to join in with him.

Behaviors other than these surely contribute to the inspiration and commitment we feel in response to visionary leaders. Most important is what these leaders try to do through their behaviors: They try to create a culture that will guide the organization through the future.

Conclusion

Over the past decade a variety of leadership research and practice work has come together to form the outline of a new vision of executive leadership. I have used the work of Elliott Jaques (on leaders' personality traits), of Talcott Parsons (on organizational culture), and of Warren Bennis (on leaders' behaviors) as the three primary elements of my theory.

Visionary leadership provides the basis for organizations that are extremely effective in terms of any criterion of performance or profit, that contribute to society a vision that benefits clients as well as the larger public, and that provides an extremely high "quality of work life" for all employees. It's hard to imagine what more one might ask of organizations . . . or leaders.

6
ENTREPRENEURIAL MANAGERS IN LARGE ORGANIZATIONS

Richard Molz

Enterprising and innovative people are the hope of the '80s, according to our business and political leaders. The focus of attention has been on entrepreneurial types in small business, however, with little recognition of the importance of entrepreneurial managers in complex, well-established organizations. Daniel Grady, Vice President of Michigan Bell, has suggested the Bell system will place a premium on people with entrepreneurial talents, to meet the needs of the firm as it restructures to comply with divestiture. Alfred Chandler in *Strategy and Structure* suggested that one of the primary roles of the top management group in any large organization is to keep the leading edge of the organization entrepreneurially sharp, to be able to seek out and seize new opportunities.

Although top management in some firms recognizes the need for nourishing entrepreneurial employees, far too many organizations, consciously or unconsciously, kill entrepreneurial talents or drive the entrepreneurial people out of the organization. Take the real case of a promising young manager, whom I will call Bill Shuler, working in a large photo products firm. Bill had demonstrated such loyalty, commitment to the company, and bright ideas at every step in his career that the firm selected him to attend an executive MBA program at the local university. Bill finished the program with flying colors and began to apply his new skills and newly generated ideas to his work as a planner and financial analyst. He soon found his ideas and interests extended beyond his particular narrow functional area and began offering them to his boss. Unfortunately, his boss was not as interested in new ideas and new ways of doing things as Bill was, and most of Bill's ideas found

Business Horizons, 27-5 (September-October 1984) pp. 54-58. Copyright 1984 by the Foundation for the School of Business at Indiana University. Reprinted by permission.

their way to the wastebasket or file cabinet, rather than into the annual business plan. Frustrated, Bill began looking for a lateral move in the organization, one that might find him working with people who were more open to new ideas and who genuinely wanted to be challenged. For whatever reasons, no such opportunities appeared to exist in the firm, and Bill eventually left for another company which seemed to offer more opportunity for someone who wanted to challenge the organization rather than merely survive long enough to collect a pension. The photo products firm had effectively driven out an innovative entrepreneur, someone who may be sorely missed in twenty years when the need for new top executives with entrepreneurial skills opens up.

Smaller organizations can also drive out entrepreneurial managers. Consider the case of Chris Morris (also a pseudonym). Chris had had the opportunity after high school to enter the family business, but the idea of wholesaling paper products to printers, publishers, office supply firms, and large organizations did not appeal to her. Interested in doing something active, Chris took Navy ROTC in college and went on to serve for several years as a Navy officer. She was assigned to a unit where she was able to lead a group of people and was given the opportunity to develop new approaches to problems. Her commanding officer listened critically but carefully to Chris when she questioned an existing procedure. After her commitment to the Navy was up, Chris was again offered a position in the family wholesaling business. The business, which was now being jointly managed by her father and her brother, was doing well in its established markets, but had done little to develop new markets or consider alternative business ventures. With mixed feelings, Chris entered the business. Careful not to offend any of the dozen or so existing employees, Chris began her new job of handling the outside portion of the business, while her brother handled the inside part of the business. With Chris on board, her father began to take more of a background role. In her specialty as outside person, Chris made it a point to get to know people in the community and to establish contact with the major clients served by the company. She soon became aware that the firm had an excellent reputation and that many existing and potential clients would become eager buyers if the firm offered some new lines or even some entirely new services. Having been trained in the Navy to demonstrate leadership and having been encouraged by her former commanding officer to offer new ideas and insights, she went to her brother and father to explore these opportunities. Their reaction was astonishment and a feeling of having been betrayed: The business was doing well as it was; why would she want to try anything new or different? Trying things new or different implied risk, and why take a risk when things are humming along smoothly?.

Bill and Chris both exhibited entrepreneurial drives in organizations that were basically resistant to change. In Bill's case the top management may have valued entrepreneurial skills, and in Chris' case her father may have himself exhibited entrepreneurial drive twenty years before, but neither Bill nor Chris were working in environments that currently valued entrepreneurial skills.

Most organizations or suborganizations within large organizations are resistant to change. They are usually characterized by having clearly defined objectives in terms of producing a product or service and are often functioning quite well at meeting these objectives. If they were not, after all, they would not be resistant to change. The manager in trouble is the one who is looking for a new way to do things.

Organizations that are resistant to change are the very ones likely to get into long-term trouble, because they have successfully stifled or driven out the entrepreneurial people who would have continuously and seriously questioned the organization's objectives. These entrepreneurial people are needed to redefine the firm's objectives to meet a changing environment full of new opportunities. This resistance to change is not to be taken lightly; it is probably something that has grown within the organization over many years. It may actually become a part of the accepted way of viewing the world; it has become a part of the essence of the organization itself. These types of organizations do not welcome executives who question the fundamental values of the organization, or who insist on looking at the changing market or competitive environment, or who develop new methods to carry out internal functions of the firm. For such organizations only the actions of outsiders (such as competitors), a serious market setback, or the introduction of competing products will result in a major change. They respond rather than initiate, drift rather than decide.

But who is this entrepreneurial person? Are entrepreneurs some wild breed of human that cannot accept the status quo and must constantly be looking for a reason to change something rather than reveling in the peace and tranquility of a profitable, smoothly functioning organization? Sometimes. And sometimes they are gamblers who bet on hunches and wild guesses. Few organizations would welcome these types of entrepreneur, but every organization needs reasonable adventurers. The organization itself must recognize the need for these rational entrepreneurial managers and must provide avenues for them to develop ideas and new approaches to prepare for the future.

Recent research at the University of Massachusetts has suggested that most chief executives view innovation as one of their most important tasks, yet one that is generally not afforded sufficient time. Technical change within our society is proceeding at an exponential rate; there are still healthy, productive Americans who were born around the time Henry Ford produced his first Model T. An organization that is resistant to change, thereby driving out entrepreneurial people, will be the least able to cope with this continuing and rapid change. For the organization to survive and flourish it must not only change, but must also incorporate mechanisms to attach itself to the concept of change. This in turn calls for systematic ways of finding and nurturing innovative people.

Can Change Makers Survive?

How can an organization adapt to entrepreneurial managers if it has been resistant to them in the past? First, some sensitivity to the behavior of entrepreneurial people is useful. Entrepreneurial people are often discontented with rules that seem arbitrary or that stifle creativity. Perhaps Bill does some of his best thinking at a noonday workout at the company gym, but then wants to eat a sparse lunch at his desk after returning to work. To Bill, the fact that he eats his lunch at his desk after the lunch hour is irrelevant; he has in fact done some of his best work during the designated lunch hour. Maybe Chris locates some of her best contacts during a mid-morning meeting of a business-women's support group, while her brother thinks of this as poor use of her time. The key with entrepreneurial people is to evaluate them on achievement of objective, or output, not on how the task is accomplished. If Bill's job is to think through managerial problems, or Chris' job is to develop new contacts, evaluate each on their performance, not on their methods.

Entrepreneurial people may generate a certain amount of discomfort in the organization. The supervisor of the entrepreneurial person will not only have to accept evaluating that person on the basis of performance, but will also be forced either to explain this new evaluation method to more traditional employees, or perhaps to begin to evaluate them on performance rather than on the old method. The entrepreneurial person will have the effect of challenging the old norms of the organization, something not always looked upon favorably by change-resistant organizations. Many people in the organization will feel threatened by an entrepreneurial manager, usually because they are most secure in their position when things are quiet and are made uneasy within a changing organization. Fearful of mistakes, they resist being evaluated on the basis of achieving outcomes. Rather, they find comfort in merely carrying out the motions of work. By age thirty-five they have had most of the entrepreneurship trained out of them. Paradoxically they have now arrived at the age and experience level when the firm must look to their group to find the entrepreneurial people needed for the top jobs. Having trained the needed skills and attitudes away, the company must now pass them over.

The entrepreneurial manager also has some responsibilities. To assure a secure place in the firm, to reduce these discomforts, and to negotiate a growing future in the company ranks, the manager needs to reaffirm frequently his or her commitment to the long-term success of the organization, even though such behavior may challenge many of its current operations, practices, and market position. It should be clear to all around that the entrepreneurial manager is functioning within the organization for the well-being of the future organization, not merely to satisfy some personal whims. The entrepreneur in the large organization either needs an odd-ball's license which allows deviant entrepreneurial behavior, or else must go undercover and innovate quietly.

The entrepreneurial manager should also be sensitive enough to deal with the discomfort of those who have long resisted any change in approach to the firm's conventions. The change maker should never attack *people* when challenging a position of the firm; the attack is upon inflexible objectives, ideas, or procedures. If one person is closely associated with a particular objective or procedure, it helps to acknowledge the past value of that perspective and to establish firmly that the environment has changed from the time it was instituted. This friendly sedition against a deadly status quo will have the effect of reducing the resistance of managers who have been closely associated with a particular program. The entrepreneurial manager, either licensed or undercover, should also be careful of attacking sacred cows, regardless of how much they may need to be attacked. Any attacks should be done with enormous care, and only after the entrepreneurial manager has established credibility within the organization. To attack a sacred cow before the young manager is established is likely to lead to early termination, or at least to a serious move backward in gaining credibility. The entrepreneurial manager in the large organization needs patience and lots of wile. Most organizations began entrepreneurially but, as a result of their success, have fallen into a mode of resistance to change. One entrepreneurial manager at lower levels will not change an organization in a week or month. Minor changes may become apparent in the first year, but major changes will take longer.

The entrepreneurial manager should become expert in the nature and forms of resistance that are a part of the essence of the bureaucratic organization. George Odiorne's book *The Change Resistors* offers an enlightening study of change-resistant organizations. Understanding this resistance will do much to help the entrepreneurial manager keep himself together in the period of underground apprenticeship, when the organization moves from being change-resistant to accepting entrepreneurial behavior from some of its employees.

Strategies for Producing Innovation

If your organization fits the model of a change-resistant enterprise and you want to produce a steady supply of innovative people to be better prepared for the continuing rapid change of the future, what can you do? First, just recognizing your organization as change- resistant is a major step. The next step is to begin to move your organization toward embracing the concept. Higher levels of management in the organization can create an innovative climate by making public statements recognizing the continuity of change or encouraging the more change-resistant subordinates to look at new ways of doing things or challenging some of the old fundamental operating assumptions on which subordinates make decisions.

Once you have begun to move the organization toward embracing change as the hope for the future rather than a nuisance to be avoided, the corporate officers can begin to review the organization's fundamental objectives. They should determine to what extent trade-offs should be made between conformity to the past, financial stability, and preparing for the future.

Lastly, corporate leaders must show active personal acceptance and support for entrepreneurial managers. This may involve reaching out to the more talented young people, listening patiently to new ideas, or objectively analyzing an idea that at first glance seems to be impossible. Many of the new ideas will be impossible or impractical. No one can hit them all on the first shot. Personal example, personal contact, and honest and open reaction, without being demeaning or discouraging, will be one of the greatest incentives a corporate officer can offer to entrepreneurial managers. You do not have to endorse every idea, but you do have to listen to every idea that is brought to you and support those that merit further consideration. Ridiculing a poor idea assures that all future ideas will be self-censored by the lesser ranks. The next one might be more worthy, but will never be heard. In the process you kill innovative talent and train entrepreneurship out of the organization.

There are four specific ways in which top management can alter the climate in their organization to permit the growth of innovation among those young people who have such tendencies. People without innovative tendencies will not form and grow them simply because it is permitted, but the creation of a climate of innovation will clear the way for those few who have such latent ability to nurture them.

- *The public statements of chiefs* can make it clear that innovation is prized and sought. Unfortunately, remote executives have less impact upon the behavior of young people buried down in the ranks than the actions of the immediate, change-resistant supervisor.
- *A goal-setting program* such as management by objectives can help, because it can indicate that innovative goals are the highest level of 1 excellence at appraisal time. Such a system will signal clearly to the entrepreneurial in the lesser ranks that their innovative behavior is not only acceptable but also desirable.
- *Reward systems* can be tailored to encourage innovation, especially from subordinates. Suggestion award systems, gain-sharing programs, and similar reward systems for innovation will produce more of it than will rewarding mere compliance with procedures. Merit increases tailored to innovation offer more than money; they offer signals to the entrepreneurs that their contributions are sought.
- *Promotional opportunities* should be reserved for the innovative and entrepreneurial, rather than for those who have just put in their time. Fast-track promotion plans, accelerated growth programs, and lists of fast-track performers can help generate a review board system of finding high talent people in the organization. The assignment of key people to identify and husband this resource and a program of early identification of the talented, entrepreneurial people are certainly within the realm of possibility for all but the most moribund bureaucracy.

The Trapped Entrepreneurial Manager

For the entrepreneurial manager who is unlucky enough to find himself in an utterly change-resistant organization, the alternatives are few. Going underground with your creative ideas or substituting agreement for creative dissent have poor track records for nurturing entrepreneurship for the organization. Nodding your head in agreement with arrant nonsense from above can become a habit and then become ingrained. Yet every effort should be made to work within the organization to convey the view that your objectives are consistent with the long-term success of the organization. If you cannot find a sympathetic ear in the immediate organization, it might be productive to look elsewhere in the organization, keeping in mind that such action will not please your immediate supervisor and may produce unfavorable consequences. Should a job change become the best alternative, either inside or outside, it is well to try to get an objective view of the nature of the organization to which you are moving. Does the new organization seem to promote new ideas and markets, or is it in the same markets it was ten years ago, using the same production technologies and the same internal control systems? If it is, and it is not consciously seeking you out as an entrepreneurial manager, you are not likely to be pleased with the new organization. Look about to find the younger people in engineering, accounting, or supervision and see if you recognize entrepreneurial, innovative people who are prospering. In the absence of such people, it might not be wise to jump from your present frying pan into the next one.

The potential entrepreneur can be found in any large organization. Top management should look for ways to spring the trap holding down these future trend-setters. These trapped underground entrepreneurs are the "can do" people of the future, and America's industrial strength was built upon just such a spirit. Our worthy foreign competitors have nothing that we do not have more of: capital, domestic market, skilled workers, and innovative leadership. While freeing the entrepreneurial urge is not a cure-all, it is one small step that will help American enterprise reassert its worldwide leadership.

7
HIGH HURDLES: THE CHALLENGE OF EXECUTIVE SELF-DEVELOPMENT

Robert E. Kaplan, Wilfred H. Drath, and Joan R. Kofodimos

Harvey was just what the board had been looking for in a CEO. He had a strong track record in turning around failing businesses, he was a marvelous strategic thinker, and he understood the company's products and markets. There was only one problem with Harvey: He was a loner. Harvey got along poorly with just about everybody. He was by turns cold and distant or downright abusive. "That's just me," Harvey once said when someone found the courage to bring this up with him. "I'm not trying to win a popularity contest here, you know." And so the company tolerated Harvey because they desperately needed his skills. He had inherited a vice-president who was good at working with others, and who began to act in Harvey's place at staff meetings and so forth. Eventually Harvey worked his managerial magic and the company turned around. A year later the board dismissed Harvey—— his abrasive personality was no longer tolerable in the smoothly running organization—and he went off to save another company. It was too bad, as it turned out, because not long after Harvey left, the company got into trouble again. They really needed Harvey and what he could do for them. A board member said of him: "Damn Harvey! We couldn't live with him and we can't live without him."

We tell this story to illustrate some of the issues of managerial development at the highest organizational levels. Perhaps the most important of these is why Harvey's organization did not try to help him improve his interpersonal ability. In general, why is it that when performance problems arise in high-level managers, the solution organizations usually prefer is to transfer, demote, or fire the executive? In effect, a game of "musical chairs" is being played in corporate executive

Reprinted by permission from The Academy of Management EXECUTIVE, 1:3 (1987), pp. 195-205.

suites.[1] Organizations may also try making up for an executive's performance problems by hiring associates with compensating strengths, but either way the solution of choice is to move (or remove) the executive or to change those around the executive; in other words, to use selection instead of development. Much less frequently do organizations attempt to create, in a manner of speaking, movement within the executive—that is, to encourage the executive's personal and managerial growth.

This paper is about self-development—the efforts of the executive to improve himself or herself, efforts that other people may well aid or hinder. By self-development we mean the conscious, deliberate effort to come to terms with one's limitations. We do not mean the kind of development that springs almost automatically from the new experiences that bring out latent abilities in the executive. We are also not concerned here with the considerable development executives have undergone on their way up.[2] Our interest is in self-aware, self-directed improvement once managers have reached the highest levels.

This paper explores the hypothesis that executives avoid coming to terms with their limitations and that the executive's organization and the people who work directly with the executive shy away from attempts to help. It is based on interviews we conducted with 40 individuals—22 executives and 18 experts on executives, including internal specialists in executive development and external consultants. The people interviewed came from a wide variety of organizations, large and small, public and private. The 40 interviews took from an hour to three hours each; this resulted in over 400 pages of interview transcripts, which we subjected to careful analysis. We were looking for patterns in what executives found problematic about their jobs, how likely it was that executives acknowledged these difficulties, and what conditions affected whether executives became aware of their problems or attempted to do something about them. For this study we defined an executive as an upper-level manager in a line position with general management responsibilities, or a high-level head of a function such as chief financial officer or vice-president of administration.[3]

Self-development is important because no executive can escape having deficits and because deficits matter to executives and their organizations. These deficits run the gamut: difficulty in thinking strategically; trouble adjusting to a job with large scope; a proclivity for viewing all problems through the lens of one's specialty;[4] discomfort with one's role as public figure and organizational spokesman; an introverted personality that people lower in the hierarchy experience as aloofness; a susceptibility to let power, position, and celebrity go to one's head; or single-minded dedication to a demanding career to the point where marriage, children, or health suffer and undermine the individual's effectiveness at work. These are the kinds of deficits we will be referring to, the deficits that can make the difference between success and failure.

Self-development is one route for dealing with an executive's deficits. It is a difficult route, one that is underutilized not just by executives but by all humans. Based on our interviews and reading, however, we have come to the conclusion that when people become executives they cross an invisible dividing line that makes self-development significantly more difficult for them. In this paper we will attempt to show just how difficult self-development is, particularly for executives—and how some of those difficulties might be overcome.

Many factors affecting self-development are present or become more pronounced as a manager moves into the executive ranks. First, executives possess power. They command formal authority, resources, access to other powerful individuals, and control over the fates of many people. Second, executives are successful. In achieving high position, most have succeeded marvelously in their careers, either by climbing the hierarchy of an existing organization or by building an organization around themselves. High-level people have also acquired expertise. They learn the business, they come to know the organization and the people in it, they become experts in managing people, solving problems, creating change, and dealing with the extraordinary demands of their jobs. There are many other factors that contribute to this special condition of being an executive, such as age, wealth, and perquisites. In addition to these elements, two personality factors were frequently mentioned during our interviews in connection with executives. One was that most executives are ambitious; they are driven to excel. The other was tied to the power and importance of the executive's role: Because doing the job involves making important decisions and affecting the lives and fortunes of others, many executives are keenly aware of a need to be highly competent and to be seen as being so.

Because our analysis showed that these elements— power, success, expertise, ambition, competence, and so forth—consistently work together to affect the executive's prospects for self-development, we shall include them all in this paper under a common descriptive term: elevation. The interrelated features of elevation are present in varying degrees in different executives and different situations. Executives are elevated to different degrees and therefore the degree to which their opportunity for self-development is impeded may vary according to the degree of elevation.

From the many interrelated features of elevation just discussed, four stand out as especially affecting the executive's prospects for self-development. For the sake of exposition, we will be treating these features separately, though in reality they act in profound concert. First, we will discuss how the exercise of power keeps executives from getting personal criticism that could lead to the awareness of deficits. Second, we examine how another route to self-awareness—introspection—is blocked by the very nature of the executive job. Third, we'll look at how the ability to accept criticism is limited by the executive's high need to be—and to appear to be—exceptionally competent. Finally, we will discuss how a history of success makes change difficult for executives. Along the way, we will also consider how some executives overcome the tendency for elevation to interfere with self-directed growth.

Power and Getting Criticism

LBJ's biographer, Doris Kearns, described the experience of being in the same room with President Johnson. "One could sense his extraordinary power," Kearns writes, "the moment he entered the room. There was a strange texture to the mere act of standing next to him; it seemed as if he were violating the physical space of those around him. . . . " (p.92)[5]

Imagine confronting such a person with his human foibles. Not very likely. We tend not to criticize the personal behavior of powerful people. Witness the following observations made by people we interviewed.

> When you're a manager, you develop a set of people you can get feedback from—a web, a grapevine, but as you rise in the hierarchy, it withers and by the time you get to the top, it's dead.

> The higher you go, the more constricted the feedback channels become.

> In most corporate organizations senior executives don't get much feedback on their weaknesses. There is not that candor in executive suites.

These are a few of many comments that lead us to recognize the fairly widespread notion that executives do not get much feedback from those around them in the organization.

We are not speaking here of the inevitable and frequent criticisms made of the decisions and policies of an executive. These appear regularly in the press and are leveled at executives from many outside interest groups. We are talking about feedback aimed not at what an executive does—the decisions he makes, the policies he formulates—but feedback aimed at how he does his job—his process of making a decision, his way of relating to others, his manner, style, behavior. In short, we are here discussing feedback aimed at the executive's modus operandi, at his managerial character. This is the kind of feedback, we found, that is impeded at the executive level. Our interviews revealed four factors related to the exercise of power that restrict feedback on executive behavior. These interrelated factors are (1) the executive's demeanor, (2) his exaggerated impact, (3) his isolation, and (4) and his relative autonomy.

The Executive's Demeanor

We found that the executive's bearing, his way of behaving around others, can inhibit feedback. This demeanor may stem from his mental acuity, his command of the issues, his history of success, or all three. Whatever its source, the demeanor of people in charge serves a useful—probably indispensable—function. A certain air of authority is no doubt necessary for executives to do their jobs. Yet no matter how necessary it is, an exaggerated, dominating presence often chokes off criticism. Clearly this is not the case with every executive. Some executives openly encourage feedback, though when this is done, the executive may still have problems convincing others of his sincerity.

In general, we found an implicit attitude in the executive's bearing that can discourage others from challenging him—especially about his management style. One executive development specialist put this attitude into words: "It's as if the executive is saying, 'I've made it to the top and one of the characteristics of being here is that the door opens one way; people don't swing my door open and tell me how to do my job.' " In other words, the executive's achievement entitles him to an exemption from advice and criticism.

In extreme cases, an executive's demeanor can cut off information brutally. Although any superior can do this to his or her subordinates, high-level managers have more power and perhaps also a greater need to exercise it. One executive we heard about would:

> . . . brook no deviation from what he perceived to be the right way to do it, which was his way. Underneath that [attitude] was an extreme temper. And he almost talked in riddles so that not only did he want control, to do it his way, but often he didn't communicate clearly to subordinates. "I don t understand what you want" was difficult for subordinates to say and even more difficult to repeat.

Such an extreme case illustrates the power of the executive's demeanor, but even in much less obvious cases there can be in the executive's demeanor an applied threat of using his position to a subordinate's disadvantage, which adds fear and resentment to the reasons that lead people to withhold criticism.

Ordinary abrasiveness can also block feedback. According to one of our sources, half the executives identified in his corporation as being "problems" were also considered "abrasive." "Zinging," as one respondent called it, usually destroys any instinct on the part of other people to help the executive with his problems, to give him constructive criticism, or to be a confidante.

To one degree or another, then, the executive's demeanor, which derives from who he is and what he does, affects the willingness of people around the executive to criticize his managerial behavior and character.

The Executive's Impact

One theme we heard again and again in our interviews centered on the executive's extraordinary impact on those around him. Many of the executives themselves brought this up as a matter of concern, especially in the area of exercising their influence. A university president told us, "If you're chief executive, people not only take what you say seriously, but they spread things around that you have simply sent up as a trial." This is characteristic of the increased sensitivity people have to the executive's words. A casual comment can reverberate with significance. An executive told us the story of seeing a picture on a subordinate's office wall. He said casually to the subordinate, "Why do you have that picture?" He was only making conversation, or so he thought. The next day when he returned to the subordinate's office he noticed that the picture had been taken away. People hang (or unhang) on every word. Comments become commands; statements become injunctions.[6] This effect can become so pronounced that some executives must guard even the expression on their faces. "If I don't smile," one told us, "people think business is bad."

The problem with this exaggerated impact is that it makes some executives reluctant to speak out at all until they are ready to make a firm decision. They become reluctant to hold casual conversations that may, they fear, turn out later not to have been so casual after all. This tends to add distance to the relationships between an executive and those around him. Keeping one's own counsel, whatever its advantages, has the effect of excluding others from involvement in, say, a decision-making process. This makes for a cooler relationship in which people feel less free to offer criticism—and in which they have less personal contact to use as a basis for criticism.

But what about "insiders," those people with whom the executive feels free to discuss issues openly, with as much speculation and "running things up the flagpole" as he wants? Are they not a valuable source of feedback? For some executives they undoubtedly are. Yet to the extent that these insiders act as "cheerleaders" for the executive, the flow of behavioral information is likely to be retarded. This can happen to any executive, even one who tries to resist it, for the simple reasons that such cheer leaders are often acting in their self-interest. They tell the executive what he wants to hear and omit what they do not want him to hear, including news of problems that might reflect badly on them.[7]

As potentially serious as this cheerleading can be, perhaps the most serious form of cheerleading is the unconscious kind, when subordinates don't withhold criticism but instead become blind to any faults in their highly placed superior. This is a form of collusion. Because of their dependency on him, subordinates cooperate with their superior in supporting the image of himself he wishes others to see.[8] By seeing the superior as he wishes to be seen, these subordinates cooperate with their superior in creating a "delusionary system.[9] Such a "delusionary system" is not likely to be fertile ground on which executives can learn and grow.

The Executive's Isolation

If the executive's demeanor cuts down on criticism and the reactions of those around the executive reduce the flow of developmentally important information, the organization also plays a part, often by its very nature. As executives move up the hierarchy, they tend to have contact with fewer and fewer people inside the organization. From his research with top executives, Burns found a "uniform segregation of three or four persons" at the top of organizations (p.60).[10] Of the time one general manager spent with people in his firm, half was spent with the other two members of his management team. As one human resources director we interviewed put it:

> I think too many top executives stay cloistered and sequestered. The people they see and the people they interact with gets narrower and narrower as they get up the pyramid.

Besides this more or less structural isolation of executives, there is an isolation that comes from insulation— the tendency of the organization to protect its executives from the indignities and problems of everyday life. Such insulation can cause the executive to lose touch with the levels below and to become increasingly unaware of much of what is going on in the company.[11]

Isolation takes a toll on communications and criticism upward because the absence of contact guarantees the absence of communication, especially of sensitive information. Moreover, the scant communication that does occur usually takes place on the executive's turf, complete with the trappings of power and the symbols of isolation, all of which can make subordinates uneasy and less comfortable about speaking up.

Executives may need to be somewhat removed to make their jobs feasible. Yet there is the counterbalancing problem: Isolation restricts criticism that an executive could use in an effort to develop and to perform his role even more effectively.

The Executive's Autonomy

Just as an executive cannot function without some isolation, neither can he function without some autonomy. We found evidence that autonomy—especially when it approaches being total, as it does in some cases—is an important factor in screening criticism of the executive's modus operandi.

Executives who have the autonomy to hire whomever they please can—and some do—often use that autonomy to hire people in their own image, people whose backgrounds, gender, and education make them compatible. Executives who do this are likely to end up with the cheerleaders we mentioned earlier, subordinates who tell them only what they want to hear.[13] From our interviews, here is a sample of comments along this line:

> Some executives are afraid to hire people with different strengths. It's a failure to trust.

> I see executives surrounding themselves with compatible people, people who fit in.

> If you rely too much on strengths, it hurts your effectiveness, and you end up hiring mirror images.

Executives are not likely to get criticism on their behavior by turning to such "mirrors."

Performance appraisal is another means by which critical information can be delivered, an institutionalized way in which organizations overcome the disinclination to give feedback about performance. But as DeVries et al. have found in their review of appraisal practices in organizations, formal appraisals thin out at high levels.[14] One consultant described the attitude of executives toward appraisal this way: "You talk about performance appraisal at the executive level? Unh-uh. That's for you folks down there." Executives can, in effect, use their autonomy to exempt themselves from having their performance assessed in this way. When executives put themselves outside the appraisal system, who but the top person is to say otherwise? The personnel executive in charge of the system ordinarily lacks the clout to define it as including the top levels, or to enforce it if the top levels merely go through the motions of participating. In granting such autonomy to its executives, an organization is allowing its executives to grant themselves an immunity to being appraised.

Getting Criticism to the Executive

Though we found that power can and often does impede criticism of the executive's managerial character, we also learned about channels that create a healthier situation for the executive, one in which he receives the critical information he needs to pursue self-development. The solutions can be grouped into those things the organizations can do, and those things that the executive himself can do.

Organizations can, for example do a lot to de-emphasize power differences. Organizations can reduce the gap between executives and others by making executive offices less impressive and locating those offices closer to those of others.[15] Intel, for example, deliberately avoids separating senior and junior people with perks such as limousines, plush offices, private dining rooms, and other status symbols.[16] If organizations segregate executives less and take away some of the trappings of power, then executives may become more accessible.

Another thing organizations can do is to create mechanisms that generate constructive criticism of executives. Standard practices such as performance appraisal are available; the issue is whether they are applied to executives. Probably the key to whether executives receive appraisals is the top executive and the extent to which that person takes the system seriously and uses it personally.

From our interviews we also learned of other mechanisms the organization can use to encourage constructive criticism. One international financial organization conducts inspections of each major unit of the organization. A member of the board of directors heads a team of three, which goes into a division and conducts confidential interviews, the results of which are channeled to the division's top management. The report includes perceptions of the CEO and the top management team. Another corporation used an outside consultant, who knew the organization and had the respect of many people in it, as a kind of ombudsman. He kept his ear to the ground and regularly fed criticism of top management back to those concerned.

People around the executive also play an important role in freeing the channels for feedback. Although they are in a distinct minority, certain individuals in the executive's world do have the inclination and courage to tell the executive about his shortcomings. One executive talked about:

> . . . the constructive critics who care enough about the organization and the person to help him and tell that person how his behavior is impacting on the organization. Those people in my executive experience are few and far between. But there are a few, and those few helped me to understand myself better.

Perhaps the most important factor is the attitude of the executive himself toward being criticized on his managerial behavior. Some executives make it a point to avoid becoming isolated and to solicit reactions to their work. More effective general managers build larger networks and make better, more skillful use of their relationships.[17] One human resources executive we interviewed commented that "the less secure [executives] really hide, but the more secure ones will step out of their offices or go down to the departments, make it a point to stay in touch." Another staff executive reported to us that people two or more levels below would never be open with him in his office, only if he went to them. We also heard from executives that they can learn what their subordinates think of them by paying close attention to cues. As one CEO put it, "You've got to learn how to read very subtle complaints." Furthermore, executives get explicit information about themselves only if they convince others of their desire for it by word and action. A CEO said: "People have to make sure they're being asked honestly, and what they are going to get back is not a 'Louisville slugger.'"

The exercise of power impedes the flow of constructive criticism, yet power must be exercised if executives are to do their jobs. So the issue is not how to reduce the power the executive needs, but how to manage those aspects of its exercise that impede criticism.

The Nature of the Job and Introspection

Another way for executives to get criticism is from themselves, through introspection. Given the problems just discussed in getting criticism from others, executives may in fact need to rely on introspection more so than lower-ranking managers. Introspection is the process of looking inward, of examining or monitoring ourselves, or trying to understand our behavior, our feelings, our defenses, our effect on others. Introspection is a necessary step in the process of self-development, whether we introspect to gain new insight about ourselves or to make sense of criticism from others. Yet the likelihood that executives will spend time and energy in introspection must be considered in light of the extraordinary demands of their work and the degree to which introspection is immediately relevant to their day-to-day performance.

Most executives are faced with staggering, unremitting demands on their time. Many of these demands rise up suddenly and urgently from sources outside the executive and beyond his control. He must respond, and can use up enormous amounts of time dealing with these demands. Although some executives—especially those at the very top—may relate to sharply reduced numbers of people within the organization, the numbers of outsiders they must relate to increases.[18] All of these demands on their time make introspection increasingly difficult.

But lack of time is not the whole story. As busy as executives are, their work lives are less hectic and unmanageable than those of some first-line supervisors, whose average day is crammed with as many as 500 discrete episodes.[19] Despite the considerable demands, executives probably enjoy greater latitude than some lower-level managers over how they spend their time.

In part the issue comes down to attitude. Executives may not find the time because introspection is not a high priority. Executives do not value introspection because it is not immediately relevant to the performance of work. The results an executive is concerned with are external and tangible—turning a plant around, improving profits, boosting productivity. Such results do not manifestly require self-understanding, and therefore do not seem to require introspection. Executives who do not see a connection between introspection and performance are understandably unwilling to give the time and energy that looking inward requires. When we asked a CEO of a small company how he looked at his performance, he said: "I look at the bottom line." Another person commented that because their commitment to the job is so high, many executives operate on a narrow sector of their personalities—one that excludes concern with self. In the same vein, Jennings asserted that executives get satisfaction from doing rather than contemplating: "Dreamers seldom make it to the top."[20] Many executives share this sense of being always immersed in action. The issue, then, is not to turn executives into navel gazers, but to help them use introspection to gain information about themselves—their behaviors, their strengths and weaknesses—so that they may develop yet more effective managerial behavior.

The Need to Be Competent and the Ability to Accept Criticism

In spite of the problems with getting criticism from others through feedback, and from themselves through introspection, executives do get criticism at times. To develop, however, we must do more than simply hear criticism; we must be able to accept its validity and, if only to ourselves, admit shortfalls in performance. As we will see, our interviews indicate a reluctance—sometimes an adamant refusal—on the part of executives to admit weakness or acknowledge any need for improvement.

We suggest that there is a relationship between the executive's reluctance to accept criticism and the executive's need to be competent. By need to be competent we mean a complex of attributes, including the need to be equal to the demands of the job, to live up to the expectations that come with high positions and to have a sense of self-worth. A number of the people we interviewed called it "ego," by which they seem to mean pride in-one's abilities and position. The need to be competent—to feel good about oneself—is something that all people have. If the executive is different it is because he carries on this struggle on a larger stage and for higher stakes.

Several factors contribute to the executive's need to be competent. One factor is the set of expectations that come with the territory, a sense that the executive must be almost larger than life. As a highly placed manager who reported to the CEO of a major corporation told us:

> [The CEO] needs to be above everybody. He needs to be smarter than everybody, never wrong. . . . He has to act [as if he were] perfect.

An internal consultant explained it this way:

> Executives in general are not supposed to have problems. They're supposed to be strong and competent and adequate to most situations.

Another factor, implied by the last quotation, is that, as holders of great responsibility, executives incur high risks. The high stakes make competent performance vitally important. Millions may be lost, lawsuits may be engendered, careers may be ruined, and jobs lost through the incompetence of a highly placed person.

Executives want to build and maintain their reputations as people who know what they are doing. The opinions they render and the policies they adopt are often highly visible and come under close scrutiny. The need to save face is therefore considerable. If executives make mistakes too often, they erode their confidence in themselves as well as the confidence of others in them. Because of this, some executives learn to be "thick skinned," they learn to protect themselves from criticism. The hitch is that they may learn this lesson too well.

The organization may cap all this by communicating its expectations of competence to the executive in powerful ways. One of the most powerful may be the special treatment that executives are accorded. Executives receive high—even exorbitantly high—salaries, are ensconced in opulent settings, and are afforded every convenience. The executive corridor typically stands as a monument to its occupants' importance.[21] As one executive said, "They sort of handle you like a precious egg." (*New York Times*, November 7, 1982) The implicit message in all of this may be that the executive had better live up to the high expectations of the organization as symbolized by the special treatment. The executive is likely to expect himself to be, and know that others also expect him to be, more than ordinarily competent.

Thus, the executive's expectations of himself and others' expectations of him can subtly—or not so subtly—nudge the executive into an unrealistic sense of his capability and importance—which in turn makes it difficult for him to hear and accept criticism. To the extent that the executive's ambition compensates for underlying doubts about himself, criticism may be unwelcome because it touches off an unconscious feeling of insecurity.

Our interviews provide support for this tendency for some executives to become unduly impressed with their competence and importance and therefore to reject criticism. A staff executive said, "Executives are susceptible to believing in their own infallibility. They think they can do no wrong." And a line executive said:

> As you grow in authority and responsibility, your confidence increases, and that can be good or bad—you can become fatuous and think you don't make mistakes.

As Hague pointed out,

> [The executive] may get conceited about his successes and blame his failure on external circumstances, but worst of all, he will cease to be self-critical and to learn from his experiences.[22]

Taken to the extreme, this can lead executives to become hypocritical, and this can be perilous. Thus, confidence turned to arrogance can be the executive's downfall.[23]

What Can Be Done?

We have talked about the tendency for executives to be tempted by an exaggerated sense of their abilities and importance, but there is nothing that says an executive must succumb. Many executives resist this temptation. In fact, their need for competence prompts them to sit tight for criticism precisely because they want to be competent. They realize they must continue learning if they are to remain competent. One executive who made a practice of examining his management style reported that at the end of the day, "I go home to my wife and say, 'I can't be that smart, I can't do everything. . . .' "

With regard to avoiding arrogance, one executive offered this advice:

> . . . absolutely most important of all for a top manager: Don't take yourself too seriously. . . . It took a lot of luck to get you the top job. You're good, but so are the people around you. Be able to laugh at yourself.[24]

By taking himself less seriously, the executive can go a long way toward reducing the loss of confidence that may come with accepting criticism. Yet we should not expect the executive to take himself lightly; he is likely always to feel the sting of criticism especially keenly. As Drucker points out, speaking of political and military leaders, "To be more [than mediocre] requires a man who is conceited enough to believe that the world . . . really needs him and depends on his getting into power.[25]

Good relations with one or more key people can help an executive overcome the temptation to reject criticism. A trusted colleague can help an executive accept negative information because there is an atmosphere of mutual respect. One executive we interviewed said:

> I'm blessed with having a very good relationship with a guy I like working with and for . . . . A key thing is mutual respect. . . . He keeps me up to date all the time on how I'm doing.

Finally, if executives are to accept criticism more readily, organizations will probably need to open the way by reducing the link between making mistakes and being judged incompetent.[26] Too often a single mistake, if large enough, brands a manager as being unequal to the task. Yet McCall and Lombardo have shown that successful managers often make many big mistakes, and that the lessons they learn from such mistakes may be critical to their success.[27] Organizations must understand—and encourage their executives to understand—that admitting weakness or ineffectiveness can be the beginning of further development and increased competence.

Success and the Motivation to Change

To become an executive one must succeed, must make the most of ability, connections, and opportunities. Managers who eventually rise to become executives are often highly regarded from the beginning and therefore well situated in the "opportunity structure."[28] These managers usually receive choice assignments in which they distinguish themselves, which leads to further opportunity to advance. This string of success followed by opportunity, opportunity followed by success, stretching over a manager's career, is what Kotter called the "success syndrome."[29] Such a career history may leave a manager well acquainted with his strengths but relatively unacquainted with his weaknesses. More important, the highly successful executive may (with some justification) feel that changing his way of managing, even a little, could hurt his chances for future success.

We found that successful managers instinctively play hands off with their style of managing. It is a conservative, sometimes superstitious attitude that is nicely encapsulated in the statement of an executive who, by changing organizations, had recently ascended to the second level of a major corporation and more than doubled his salary in the process: "Fundamentally, my management style is cast, and I'm not about to risk changing it and jeopardize the success I've achieved." Successful people see no reason to tamper with a winning formula. As a staff executive said, "[Successful executives] adapt as little as possible. What's gotten them there has been successful, so why change it?"

Many successful executives may be worried, perhaps rightly so, about losing their effectiveness if they change. This anxiety may be coupled with a general fear of failure that researchers such as Jennings have noted in executives—an anxiety that they will not accomplish what they want.[30] A consultant we interviewed described an executive who was afraid of losing effectiveness:

> The person is cautious about changing, saying that he knows his organization talks about a more humanistic approach, a greater emphasis on human relationship skills, but "if I lose some of my toughness, am I really going to be successful?"

Rather than correcting deficiencies, successful executives seem more interested in building on strengths. We interviewed a rising young executive who, for example, as was obvious from the way he expressed himself, excelled at conceptualizing and communicating. But when we asked him whether he tried to develop himself as a manger, the two things he mentioned as developmental targets were analytical ability and communication, just those things he already did well. Although building on strengths can be an effective developmental approach, if it becomes a substitute for correcting deficiencies, if an executive is developmentally satisfied merely to get better at what he or she is already good at, then weaknesses will remain, and they may eventually outweigh the strengths. Building on strengths is the kind of change people generally find comfortable; correcting weaknesses is risky and painful.

Is it success itself that makes change difficult for executives? Isn't the reluctance to change just human nature? Our interviews suggest that success is indeed a significant factor. As one management consultant observed:

> I've worked with people on a lower management rung all the way up to the people at high levels and certainly the people who are lower are much more willing to look at themselves. They're still trying to find their leadership style, define what's going to lead to success in their organizations.

As these managers become more successful, their motivation to change can diminish. An executive with many years of experience said of people on the fast track that:

> There's a certain crown prince image they're conscious of. So I'd say, in a number of cases, they feel that they've made it and all they have to do is to continue to do the things they've done in the past and they will rise to even greater heights.

How Do Executives Change?

Executives change for the same reasons that anyone changes— because they want to or have to. The motivation to perform well impels executives to pursue their own development. Said one CEO: "I know I must keep growing. What worked yesterday might not work tomorrow." So executives whose urge to be effective is strong enough to offset the forces that exert a drag on executive self-development will cultivate their own development. One group vice-president we heard about started each year by giving his immediate subordinates his agenda for personal change for the coming year. By making his plans public, he committed himself to change.

When the individual executive will not pursue needed change on his own, then an option is for other people to step in and press for change. Alcoholics represent a classic case of executives who have problems that they usually don't solve voluntarily. The task of penetrating these layers of rationalization with which alcoholics surround themselves may require as drastic a step as surprise confrontation. A Richardson-Vicks Inc. executive found himself confronted by the company medical director and colleagues critical of his performance who told him to attend a treatment program or lose his job. He went to the program.[31] This type of confrontation precipitates the crisis to which the executive is inevitably headed. It motivates the executive by threatening him with the loss of his job if not his career.

To overcome stiff resistance to change, it takes manufactured crises like these—or the naturally occurring ones, like actual career failure or life crises, which in one fell swoop can penetrate consciousness, command acceptance, and touch off an effort to change. A personal crisis, such as a divorce or death of a loved one, can provoke an executive to question himself and his priorities: "Sometimes there's a precipitating event . . . that makes executives in retrospect look at the whole trip they've been on." Even someone else's trouble, when it hits close to home, can encourage learning. One consultant to executives describes a typical reaction to a co-worker being fired; "I thought he was safe and he just got shot down. Am I next? Maybe I'd better not have those blind spots."

Conclusion

In a study related to ours, McCall and Lombardo found that one of the things that seems to make the difference between success and failure at the top is a capability to overcome the obstacles we have been discussing and engage in self-directed growth.[32] In that study, both the executives who remained successful after reaching the top and those who derailed had flaws; part of what distinguished the two groups was how individuals dealt with their flaws. Drawing on the original data of this study, we found, for example, a derailed executive who "would never believe he had interpersonal problems." He took the attitude that: "After 28 years no one can question my performance." In contrast to such a posture, the successful executives in that study remained sufficiently courageous to acknowledge their faults and do something about them.

To recognize a problem of one's own making corresponds closely to the flexible defense-and-adaptation mechanisms used by the successful cases in George Vaillant's longitudinal study of 100 Harvard graduates. In the face of duress or crisis, the successes—well adapted and mentally healthy people—responded neither by denying the problem nor by fighting it. Rather, they managed by themselves and with the help of their friends to absorb the shock of the difficulty and work through it.[33] Zaleznik reported that how creative people manage disappointment is a key to the evolution of their careers. If they face a catalytic psychological event, then they grow as people and professionals. If they deny it, then growth is retarded because the unresolved conflicts remain.[34]

The best use of self-analysis and self-redirection is in response to a specific need: a setback at work, repeated difficulties at one's job, a career impasse, a transition to radically different responsibilities, a crisis at home, or a build-up of health-threatening stress. Self development is one effective way to come to terms with transitions, crises, setbacks, or persistent tension from any source. People with a sense of well-being "take time for critical self-reflection only when approaching a tough transition or after making one."[35] Introspection peaks at time of transition and drops to low levels at other times. Executives who react to being plateaued, demoted, or terminated by immediately finding another job and scrupulously avoiding any self-scrutiny are setting themselves up for a repetition of the same problem in their next job.

There is an irony in all of this. The executive whose power, impact, access to resources, experience and skill, and wealth, social position, and success all work to set him above most of his fellow humans and grant him the means to influence and accomplish great things may find more difficulty than most in knowing himself, and he is constrained by his condition from the fullest development of his capabilities. In human, organizational, and societal terms, and despite the obstacles that impede it, self-development for executives is a frontier worth exploring.

Notes

1. See, for example, P. O'Toole, *Corporate Messiah: The Hiring and Firing of Million-Dollar Managers.* New York: William Morrow & Co., 1984.

2. There is a growing body of literature on this subject, including the following: D. W. Bray, R. J. Campbell, and D. L. Grant, *Formative Years in Business: A Long-Term AT&T Study of Managerial Lives.* New York: Wiley-Interscience, 1974; W. Bennis, *The Unconscious Conspiracy: Why Leaders Can't Lead.* New York: AMACOM, 1976; E. H. Schein, *Career Dynamics: Matching Individual and Organizational Needs.* Reading, MA: Addison-Wesley, 1978; and M. M. Lombardo, M. W. McCall, Jr., A. M. Morrison, and R. P. White, "Key Events and Learnings in the Lives of Executives." In M. Lombardo (Chair), *Key Events and Learnings in the Lives of Executives.* Symposium presented at the 43rd Annual Meeting of the Academy of Management, Dallas, 1983.

3. All the executives we interviewed and described in the interviews were men. In generalizing from these interviews, we therefore limit our remarks to male executives and use the masculine pronouns exclusively. Also for information regarding this study, a longer version is available from the Center for Creative Leadership, 500 Laurinda Drive, P.O. Box P-1, Greensboro, NC 27402-1660.

4. J. J. Gabarro, "When a New Manager Takes Charge." *Harvard Business Review* 1986, 63(3), 110-123.

5. D. Kearns, "Angels of Vision." In M. Pachter (Ed.), *Telling Lives: The Biographer's Art*. Washington, D.C.: New Republic Books, 1979.

6. See R. D. Laing, *Self and Others*. London: Penguin, 1967, for a psychological exposition of this power phenomenon.

7. See, for example, W. H. Read, "Upward Communication in Industrial Hierarchies." *Human Relations* 1962, 15, 3-15; and T. Burns and G. M. Stalker, *The Management of Innovation*. London: Social Science Paperback, Tavistock Publications, 1961.

8. E. Goffman, *The Presentation of Self in Everyday Life*. Garden City, NY: Doubleday, 1959.

9. M. F. R. Kets de Vries, "Managers Can Drive Their Subordinates Mad." *Harvard Business Review* 1979, 57(4), 125-134.

10. T. Burns, "Management in Action." *Operational Research Quarterly* 1957, 8(2), 45-60.

11. For a brief discussion of this "losing touch" behavior, see R. Townsend, "Further Up the Organization." *New Management* 1984, 1(4), 6-11.

12. F. Steele, "The Ecology of Executive Teams: A New View of the Top." *Organizational Dynamics* 1983, 11(4), 65-78.

13. The following authors have highlighted this problem: A. Zaleznik and M. F. R. Kets de Vries, *Power and the Corporate Mind*. Boston: Houghton Mifflin, 1975; W. Bennis, *The Unconscious Conspiracy: Why Leaders Can't Lead*. New York: AMACOM, 1976; and R. M. Kanter, *Men and Women of the Corporation*. New York: McGraw-Hill, 1977.

14. D. L. DeVries, A. M. Morrison, M. G. Gerlach, & S. L. Shullman, *Performance Appraisal on the Line*. New York: John Wiley & Sons, 1981.

15. See Steele, Endnote 12.

16. A. S. Grove, "Breaking the Chains of Command (My Turn)." *Newsweek*, October 3, 1983.

17. J. P. Kotter, *The General Mangers*. New York: The Free Press, 1982.

18. R. Dubin & S. L. Spray, "Executive Behavior and Interactions." *Industrial Relations* 1964, 3, 99-108.

19. M. W. McCall, Jr., A. M. Morrison, and R. L. Hannan, *Studies of Managerial Work: Results and Methods* (Tech. Rep. 9). Greensboro, NC: Center for Creative Leadership, 1978.

20. E. E. Jennings, *The Executive in Crisis*. New York: McGraw-Hill, 1965.

21. See Steele, Endnote 12.

22. H. Hague, *Executive Self-Development: Real Learning in Real Situations*. New York: Wiley, 1974.

23. M. W. McCall, Jr., and M. M. Lombardo, *Off the Track: Why and How Successful Executives Get Derailed* (Tech. Rep. 21). Greensboro, N.C.: Center for Creative Leadership, 1983.

24. E. J. Cattabiani and R. White, "Participative Management." *Issues & Observations*, August, 1983, 3(3), 1-6 (A Center for Creative Leadership publication).

25. P. F. Drucker, *The Effective Executive*. New York: Harper & Row, 1966.

26. T. J. Peters and R. H. Waterman, Jr., *In Search of Excellence*, New York: Harper & Row, 1982.

27. See McCall and Lombardo, Endnote 23.

28. See Kanter, Endnote 13.

29. See Kotter, Endnote 17.

30. See Jennings, Endnote 20.

31. R. S. Greenberger, "Sobering Method: Firms are Confronting Alcoholic Executives with Threat of Firing." *Wall Street Journal*, January 13, 1983, p. 1.

32. See McCall and Lombardo, Endnote 23.

33. G. E. Vaillant, *Adaptation to Life*. Boston: Little, Brown, & Co., 1977.

34. A. Zaleznik, "Management of Disappointment." In E. G. C. Collins (Ed.), *Executive Success: Making It in Management*. New York: John Wiley & Sons, 1983, pp. 226-244.

35. G. Sheehy, *Pathfinders*. New York: William Morrow & Co., 1981.

PART 3
STYLE AND
SUBSTANCE

What leaders do is important, but how they do it is even more important. Substance relates directly to organizational outcomes. Style reflects the process by which the leader interacts with others to get the job done. It is one thing to complete a task, but how people feel about what they have accomplished also has significant meaning.

Much of the research in leadership has focused on style. The two most common references are to the autocratic and democratic behaviors, the latter representing a more collaborative or participative approach. Whether the leader accomplishes the task is important to both styles. Over the years, shared leadership has been more popular because of the long-term effects on the people in an organization. Ownership of the solutions and implemented process seem to provide participants with greater personal satisfaction and commitment to the organization.

Because we are talking about personality, the issue of style is more than one type versus another as the one best for all situations. The task, for example, is an important consideration. The more complex or ambiguous the task, the greater the need to have a variety of inputs. Relatively simple, routine tasks can often be directed by a leader acting alone. But style is not related only to task.

Timing is also important. Participative styles are time consuming. Shared leadership includes subordinates, and the path to consensus decisions is often long and tedious. In situations where quick decisions are necessary for survival, the leader must act on available information and make the decision. Participation depends on the time demands placed on the leader and subordinates.

Leader Behaviors

Increased interest in leadership has spawned a variety of "how to" books providing formulas for success. By describing the deeds of those in charge of successful organizations, writers attempt to list those qualities "necessary" for successful leadership. Some of the more common attributes are:

■ Vision
■ Communicating (articulating) the vision
■ Inspiring others to achieve that vision

- Creativity in developing action strategies
- Commitment to the organization and the task
- Loyalty to the people in the organization

But how does one develop those skills? More importantly, it is not clear that these are skills at all. There is no set pattern of activities, no single path to leadership. Over a period of time, a successful organization can be led by individuals with very different personalities and styles. Leaders can move from one organization to another and succeed or fail, even though his or her style remains constant. Finally, there is no universal set of characteristics.

Effective leaders seem to behave in ways that fit their personalities, the situation, and the needs of the group that they are leading. In a sense, they act naturally. While there is an empathy with the group, the leader presents himself or herself with self-knowledge and confidence. There is no set of acquired behaviors to play a role. One cannot pretend a dynamic, enthusiastic commitment to leadership.

Some leaders take charge. Others nurture the group so that everyone accepts responsibility. We know leaders who are great orators. There are also those who are quiet and uninspiring with words but who lead by example. Leaders come in all statures and from all cultures. Some act decisively; others act with slow deliberation. The key is that the effective leader sets the stage with his or her personality and expectations, presenting a consistent image.

Performance and Outcomes

We evaluate leaders in terms of their personal effectiveness and the organization goals. Sales, profits, employment, and equity changes are the tangible measures applied to organizational success or failure. There are many reports at frequent intervals, supplying a continuous evaluation of leader effectiveness.

There are intrinsic and extrinsic outcomes to leadership. Apart from the organization measurement systems, the leader has a feeling about what has been done. There is an ego involvement; leaders are an integral part of the situation. They are continually engaged in a self-evaluation because, to a leader, making a difference is what's important.

The role the leader chooses to play (or is expected to play) also relates to effectiveness. There is the role of figurehead or spokesperson. In this capacity, the leader is a communicator who represents the goals and values of the organization to the outside world. Or a leader can choose to focus internally, being a buffer with the external environment and concentrating his or her efforts on actions within the organizational boundaries. The leader can elect to be the storyteller, working primarily to inspire members to work toward a common objective. Many people lead by example, being the hardest worker and making the sacrifices that create an energizing environment for all to contribute.

Again, we come to the issue of personality. Who the leader is, in large part, determines the nature of the role. One must make a conscious, determined choice to become a great communicator. Hard work and commitment cannot be simulated. At the same time, what an organization *needs* is critical. If internal restructuring is needed, we look for leaders who can direct their energies to that end. We cannot expect leaders to respond equally well to every shift in organizational emphasis. There are some people who can adapt well as leaders. Effective leaders know their strengths and weaknesses and act accordingly.

Transactional leaders recognize what participants want to get from their work and try to see that they get it if warranted by their performance—exchanging rewards (and promises of rewards) for effort.

The leader recognizes the role the follower must play to attain outcomes desired by the leader. Roles are clarified, giving participants the confidence necessary to achieve the goals. At the same time, the leader recognizes what the participants need, clarifying (for the participants) how those needs can be fulfilled in exchange for satisfactory effort and performance. Properly implemented, transactional leadership is effective and desirable for appropriate situations.

Transformational leadership involves strong personal identification with the leader, joining in a shared vision of the future—going beyond self-interest and exchange of rewards for compliance. The transformational leader motivates participants to perform *beyond* expectations by:

- Creating a shared awareness of the importance and value of designated outcomes
- Influencing followers to transcend their own self-interest
- Altering or expanding participant motivations to the higher orders of self-esteem and self-actualization

Through the use of language, a transformational leader helps participants develop a mental picture of the vision and transforms purpose into action.

Context

There have always been barriers to leadership. Some reflect current attitudes of society while others are inherent in the nature of organizations. Critics contend that any barriers are simply perceived, but we act on our perceptions; these barriers have been real to the individuals involved.

Leaders must be accepted by those who want to be led. Whether that acceptance is determined by force, a form of economic exchange, or moral suasion, there is a bond established by the leader and group that permits movement to take place. This is the legitimacy of the leader in his or her role.

At the same time, there must be an established role for the leader to play. Often, this is at the head of an organization, formally established and associated with specific responsibilities and authority. Informal leadership may exist independently of the organization structure, but there are standards and expectations for leader behaviors. Some organizations are open to leadership while others restrict access and effectiveness.

The real dilemma is understanding whether one is constrained in exercising leadership because of limited opportunities (organizational) or by lack of self-confidence (individual). Do minorities and women have *access* to leadership roles? Serious discussions on affirmative and negative responses make it hard to come to any conclusions. Moreover, there are questions as to whether everyone has the same opportunities for leadership development. As our institutions change, we need to explore the nature of any barriers.

Everyone Has Potential

We believe that everyone has the potential to be a leader. Self-knowledge is a personal endeavor, and we all have the opportunity to explore who we are and what we believe. There are formal courses as well as the ability to design one's own course of study. The only hurdle is to want the understanding of self. It is not easy to ask ourselves the hard questions.

Who am I?
What are my strengths and weaknesses?
Where am I going?
What are my values?
and the list goes on. . . .

These are questions that we should not ask unless we are ready to accept the answers. More importantly, we must accept the answers and be comfortable and confident in them.

Are there issues of gender and race that limit one's leadership potential? Yes, perhaps, but what they are is not clear. Our society has gone through a great deal of change. On the one hand, minorities and women are being encouraged to seek leadership positions in increasing numbers. They are being encouraged and nurtured in a variety of ways. On the other hand, we see very few minorities and women in important leadership roles. The numbers are increasing, but they do not reflect our intentions. It may be a "pipeline" problem as our organizations catch up with changing attitudes and a true commitment to equal opportunity. Or, it may be a manifestation of restricted access.

Leadership Perspectives

In the series of articles that follows, we present some compelling cases for many different styles of leadership. In each case, substance is determined by the needs of the organization. Effectiveness is the key: How does the leader make a difference in the organization as the members accomplish their collective goals and objectives?

Muczyk and Reimann present a very unusual argument in "The Case for Directive Leadership." With all the attention given to collaborative leadership styles, this approach is given merit in terms of the organization's needs as well as the individual leader's. The endnotes expand this piece in important ways.

A complementary piece by Peter Drucker follows. In "Leadership: More Doing Than Dash," he talks less about personality ("charisma") and more about performance. The notion of misleaders is an interesting perspective. While his examples are masculine, the issues are not gender specific. To Drucker, it is not who the leader is; it is what he or she *does* that matters.

Bernard Bass combines charisma with substance in "Leadership: Good, Better, Best." This is the transformational leadership model. While he admits that this style is not appropriate for all circumstances, he does suggest that we need to pay more attention to the qualities of charisma, individualized consideration, and intellectual stimulation.

In "Dancing on the Glass Ceiling," Regina Herzlinger presents a provocative essay on female leadership in today's organizations. Problems of access for minorities and women are widely reported and analyzed. What is wrong prevails as a theme. We decided to advance Herzlinger's perspective to stimulate thoughts in another direction.

We conclude this section with Thomas Horton's "Qualities of a Successful CEO." His description of the common characteristics of effective business leaders captures the leader-manager issue while integrating style and substance.

There is no doubt that what a leader does is essential to the success or failure of the organization. Equally important to the people in that organization and to the long-term success of the enterprise is the way in which the leader creates the impetus for action. It is not style *or* substance; both make the important difference.

8
THE CASE FOR DIRECTIVE LEADERSHIP

Jan P. Muczyk and Bernard C. Reimann

Gerry Gladstone still doesn't know what hit him. After a little over a year as president of Allied Machinery Company he's out looking for a job again. Things started out so well, too! When Allied's board first offered him the job as president, Gerry was delighted. He had always wanted the opportunity to run his own show. And with his prior experience as the general manager of the Machinery Division of a large conglomerate, he was confident that he could turn the smaller firm around. He felt that he had learned just about everything he needed to know about running a company while rising through the ranks of his previous employer. Moreover, his division had been one of the most profitable in the corporation, and particularly adept in competing against Allied. No wonder Allied's board had high hopes that Gerry would be able to turn their company around.

Unfortunately things haven't worked out quite that way. A year later Allied is still doing quite poorly and hasn't even been able to get its share of the substantial increase in its industry's sales. Why was a manager with a proven record and impeccable credentials unable to work his accustomed magic in his new position? What Gerry found out, much to his chagrin, was that he had been "spoiled" in his previous management positions.

Without fully realizing it, Gerry had come to count on the superior quality subordinates and organizational support systems that had allowed him to leverage his own management talents. He had learned how to make the most of his organization's substantial resources through extensive delegation and employee participation. What's more, his democratic leadership style, which had come quite naturally to an

Reprinted by permission from The Academy of Management EXECUTIVE, 1:4 (1987), pp. 301-311 idealistic MBA graduate in the late '60s, was subsequently reinforced by considerable success in this early business career. He had literally come to believe that there was no other way to manage. When Gerry took over as president of Allied, he faced an environment that differed radically from the one to which he had grown accustomed. First of all, most of the managers reporting to him did not have nearly the capabilities of initiative of his former subordinates. They were used to being told what to do and then having the boss follow up closely to make sure they were doing it right. Small wonder that Gerry's participative and delegative style was foreign to these executives and resulted in more confusion than action!

To make matters worse, Allied did not have most of the well developed support systems, from basic organizational procedures like order processing and inventory control to sophisticated information systems that Gerry had learned to use so well. As a result, he was unable to get the kinds of results that had come so naturally in his previous management posts. Without the accustomed guidance and follow-up of their boss, his new subordinates simply failed to carry out their assigned tasks properly or on time. And, lacking any standard procedures and reliable control systems, Gerry didn't discover many of these failures until too late. Instead of the expected improvement in Allied's performance, things went from bad to worse in several critical areas. The board, understandably disappointed with these results, finally asked Gerry to resign.

Why Participative Management May Not Work

While the names are fictitious, the above scenario is not. What's more, similar events are taking place all over the country, in a wide variety of organizational settings. This common scenario illustrates the danger of concluding that the "best" or "excellent" style of leadership is a participative or democratic one. Like Gerry Gladstone, many managers have been forced to face the harsh reality that participative management simply may not work in some situations. Leadership is a two-way street, so a democratic style will be effective only if followers are both willing and able to participate actively in the decision-making process. If they are not, the leader cannot be democratic without also being "directive" and following up very closely to see that directives are being carried out properly.

In spite of its practical importance, direction has not received the attention it deserves in the leadership literature. This slight is due, in part at least, to a common failure to distinguish between the direction and participation dimensions of leadership. Some writers have even implied that direction is the opposite of participation, making directive leadership appear somehow un-democratic and even un-American.

In this article we intend to show that directive leadership is not inconsistent with participation. On the contrary, directiveness may be regarded as a separate dimension of leadership style in its own right—one that complements, but does not negate, participative management. What's more, the combination of the direction and participation dimensions can be helpful in reconciling some of the conflicting theories and research about whether a particular style of leadership is "best" for managers in various situations. The combination of these two dimensions can also be used to describe four "generic" leadership styles and the circumstances under which each is most likely to be effective.

What Is Leadership

In his classic book, *The Nature of Managerial Work*, Henry Mintzberg identified ten managerial roles: (1) figurehead, (2) leader, (3) liaison, (4) monitor, (5) disseminator, (6) spokesman, (7) entrepreneur, (8) disturbance handler, (9) resource allocator, and (10) negotiator. Leadership, as we use the term in this article, concerns the leader role as Mintzberg defined it. This role describes the relationship between the manager and subordinates that results in the satisfactory execution of subordinates' assignments and, thereby, the attainment of the important goals of the organizational unit for which the leader is responsible. What's more, we agree with Mintzberg's contention that providing leadership is the most important of the ten managerial roles.[1]

The importance of leadership is also reflected in the substantial body of literature dealing with this subject. Several thousand articles and books have been published in the last two decades that deal with one aspect or another of leadership.[2] The result has been a veritable jungle of theories and often conflicting results and advice. Some of the best known approaches to the study of leadership include: (1) trait theories (Ghiselli); (2) personal-behavioral theories (University of Michigan and Ohio State studies); (3) situational or contingency theories (Tannenbaum and Schmidt, Fiedler, and Vroom); (4) path-goal theory (House); and (5) vertical dyad linkage theory (Graen).[3] One result of the profusion of theories about leadership has been a great deal of uncertainty about the most effective ways for managers to lead their subordinates. While the leadership controversy is grist for the academician's mill, it is pure poison for the practitioner. Managers can't afford to investigate or debate the pros and cons of various theories. They must have straightforward solutions with demonstrated success.

This need for simple, sensible, and proven answers may account for much of the current excitement about participative leadership. First of all, the idea of participation in the workplace is intuitively appealing in a democratic society well populated with "60's kids."[4] Second, the success of progressive practices like participative management in "excellent" companies like IBM, 3M, or HP has been widely publicized in recent years.[5] It is very tempting to say that what's good for these paragons of excellence must be good for any organization that wants to emulate their success.

However, we must not lose sight of the fact that the bulk of our leaders are found in organizations that provide less than "excellent" environments for the exercise of participative leadership. The relatively low profile of these much more numerous "average" organizations, along with our country's strong democratic roots, may have resulted in some overexposure and even overselling of participative leadership.[6]

If participative management is to be more than just a popular "fad," its alleged superiority has to be supported by well designed empirical research. This does not yet appear to be the case. For every study reporting higher group performance for participative managers relative to more autocratic ones, others have found either worse performance or no difference at all. A careful review of the classic studies of worker participation also suggests that the relationship between participation and performance is much more complex than generally assumed. Many leadership studies have been flawed by their apparent failure to consider the effects of important variables such as the characteristics of followers or other aspects of the situation.[7]

Participation vs. Direction

One explanation for the inconsistent results from leadership research is that the impact of participation may have been confounded in at least some studies by a tendency to regard decision making and execution as one and the same. To appreciate how direction both differs from and complements participation, the act of making a decision needs to be separated from the process of executing it. Participation is associated with making a decision, while direction is concerned with executing a decision once it has been made. Democratic or participative leadership is typically defined in terms of the degree to which employees are involved in significant day-to-day, work-related decisions. However, the participation of employees in making decisions is a separate issue from the amount of direction that a leader provides in executing those decisions. Thus, a leader can be participative or democratic by consulting employees during the decision-making phase, yet still be directive by following up closely on progress toward the ends that have been mutually decided on. This is illustrated in the two scales below.

Participation

| (Autocratic) | Low _____ High | (Democratic or participative) |

Direction

| (Permissive, general supervision) | Low _____ High | (Directive, close supervision, constant follow up) |

Autocratic leaders take the position that they are paid to make key decisions and the subordinates are compensated for executing those decisions. Thus, subordinates are not involved in decision making under pure autocratic leadership. Democratic leaders, on the other hand, believe in the legitimacy of subordinate involvement in decision making, even though they may retain the authority to make the final decision. Participation does not mean the mere solicitation of inputs from subordinates, which are then ignored. Yet, on occasion, circumstances may dictate that the recommendations of subordinates need to be reversed. At times subordinates may even have to be excluded entirely from a decision. However, a truly participative leader feels obligated to explain to subordinates why their counsel had to be rejected.

Directive behavior is a function of the way the leader delegates the tasks associated with the execution of a decision, once it is made. A nondirective or permissive leader holds followers responsible for results, but leaves them free to execute their tasks in any way they choose. A very directive leader, on the other hand, specifies how subordinates are to accomplish their assignments and then follows up closely on all phases of the actual execution as well as the end results.

It is worth noting that both participation and direction involve aspects of delegation. Participation concerns the degree to which the leader lets subordinates take on some of the responsibility for making decisions about which tasks, projects, or results are to be achieved. Direction reflects the extent to which the leader delegates the responsibility for choosing the actual means to accomplish the desired tasks, projects, or results.

Dimensions of Leadership

Of course, participation and direction are not the only dimensions of leadership style. A close look at the literature reveals that researchers have considered at least three other major dimensions. The most common labels for these three dimensions and some of their synonyms are:

1. *Consideration* (concern for people; good human relations)
2. *Concern for production* (goal emphasis; achievement orientation)
3. *Incentive for performance* (performance-reward connection)

Consideration and Concern for Production

Blake and Mouton's "Managerial Grid" has become a favorite leadership model—especially among practitioners. This grid is a loosely in terpreted application of the Ohio State leadership research and focuses on the two dimensions of "concern for people" (consideration) and "concern for production." This model is a normative one, since the goal for any organization is to be high on both dimensions. That is, Blake and Mouton advise managers to work toward the highest, "9,9" leadership style in their organizations.[8]

We certainly have no quarrel with that advice; common sense, as well as research, suggest that treating subordinates with concern and respect, as well as demonstrating a strong desire for goal achievement, are essential to effective leadership in the workplace. Since high "consideration" is really nothing more than sound human relations, so it should undergird any effective leadership style.

A clear goal emphasis, or achievement orientation, should also be part of an effective leadership style in any goal-oriented organization. Blake and Mouton's "concern for production" implies that a leader emphasizes output, quality, meeting deadlines, living within the budget, minimizing scrap, and so on. That is, the leader's concern for production is reflected in an emphasis on the attainment of results.[9]

Incentive for Performance

Successful leaders also make every effort to strengthen the connection between performance and rewards. Research evidence indicates that incentive pay systems increase productivity between 15 and 35 percent.[10] The incentives offered also must clear a motivational threshold, if they are to have a significant impact on performance. Employees will take their pay in the form of leisure rather than exert maximum effort for an extra five or ten cents an hour. Many organizations severely limit their leaders' options for rewarding individual performance. Nevertheless, leaders often have some latitude to link performance to rewards. This is especially true for the nonmonetary variety—such as favorable job assignments and lavish praise. The extent to which the leader links available rewards or sanctions to subordinate performance defines a leadership dimension that we call "incentive for performance." This leadership dimension is a fundamental part of path-goal leadership theory.[11] In keeping with this theory, as well as our own research and practical experience, we propose that leaders should create the strongest connection possible between performance and rewards (or sanctions) that organizational constraints will permit.

Which Leadership Style is "Best?"

A fundamental controversy in the leadership literature revolves around the existence or nonexistence of "one best style of leadership?" The normative school supports the notion that the most effective style is generalizable to all leadership situations. In direct contrast, the situational or contingency theorists believe that the effectiveness of a given leadership style is a function of the situation.[12] We feel that these arguments may be largely futile because the two camps have been concerned with important, but entirely different, aspects of leadership. Therefore, we propose a new way of relating and reconciling these apparently different points of view. What emerges from this reconciliation is a set of fresh guidelines for the use of participative and directive leadership behaviors.

Much of the normative research has focused on the three dimensions of consideration, concern for production, and incentive for performance. Furthermore, the normative findings are borne out by the management practices of excellent companies like IBM, 3M, and General Electric. These firms all emphasize sound human relations, high achievement levels, and rewards tied to performance. Therefore, we suggest that managers should earn and maintain high marks on all three of the above dimensions, regardless of the circumstances. That is, high concern for both people and production, coupled with strong incentives for performance, are necessary in any situation that calls for the accomplishment of goals through organized effort.

However, high scores on these three factors are insufficient for the most effective exercise of leadership. In keeping with the view of contingency theorists, these three dimensions need to be augmented by the proper display of participative and directive leader behaviors, as called for by different situations. In other words, the effectiveness of participative and directive leader behaviors depends on the situation in which leadership is to be exercised. Thus, the answer to the question "Which leadership style is best?" is still "It all depends!" However, we can simplify the situational contingencies since we have reduced our critical factors down to the two that are most sensitive to changes in the leadership environment.

Types of Leader Behavior

If leaders are classified as either high or low on participation and direction, we come up with the four sets of leader behaviors illustrated in Figure 8.1. We have labeled the types of leaders exhibiting these four patterns of behavior as follows: (1) the directive autocrat, (2) the permissive autocrat, (3) the directive democrat, and (4) the permissive democrat. We will briefly describe each of these and identify the circumstances under which each type of leader would be most likely to be successful.

Fig. 8.1. Types of Leader Behaviors

Degree of Participation in Decision Making:

		Low	High
Amount of Leader Direction:	High	Directive Autocrat	Directive Democrat
	Low	Permissive Autocrat	Permissive Democrat

The Directive Autocrat

This is the type of leader who makes decisions unilaterally and also supervises the activities of subordinates very closely. Directive-autocratic leaders would suit situations that require quick action, with no time for extensive employee participation. They would also be effective in an organization or subunit with limited scope or size and with relatively unstructured tasks. The low degree of delegation, coupled with extensive follow up, would overburden the leader in larger more complex organizational units. The directive autocrat is particularly well suited to lead new, inexperienced, or under-qualified subordinates. This type of leader may also be required if subordinates are in an adversarial relationship to management, and must be constantly coerced to do their work. However, the directive autocrat must be very knowledgeable in all aspects of the unit's mission and be comfortable in an autocratic role.[13]

An example of a situation that calls for a directive autocrat would be the small, entrepreneurial firm operating in a dynamic, competitive environment with new or inexperienced employees. The entrepreneur knows the business inside and out, must make quick decisions, and cannot (or will not) trust employees to operate without close follow-up.

A directive autocrat may also be the type of leader needed in large organizations producing a homogeneous product with simple technology. As long as Coca Cola remained a one-product company, the directive and autocratic behaviors of J. Paul Austin and his predecessor, Robert W. Woodruff, served the company well. Once Coca-Cola diversified into the entertainment and food industries, and decentralized geographically (53% of operating profit comes from overseas), the more democratic and permissive behavior, as exemplified by the current CEO, Roberto C. Goizueta, was called for.[14]

The Permissive Autocrat

This type of leader still makes decisions alone, but permits followers a great deal of latitude in accomplishing their delegated tasks. The permissive autocrat would also be well suited for situations calling for quick responses. However, the tasks should be relatively simple and structured, or employees should have good experience, ability, and initiative. While still autocratically inclined, this permissive leader trusts subordinates to carry out their orders without constant follow-up. Or, this permissiveness may simply reflect an unwillingness to take the time needed for extensive follow-up.

At first glance, permissiveness and autocracy don't seem to be compatible. After all, what self-respecting autocrat would take the risk of losing control over the activities and outputs of subordinates? Autocratic managers have to be sure that their directives are followed. Therefore, they cannot afford to be permissive unless they have access to some sort of substitute for personal direction. A wide variety of such substitutes can be found, but some of the more common ones include well-defined or routine tasks, technology, incentive systems, professional standards, or a strong corporate culture.

One example of a situation requiring little personal direction is a department with a highly routine task in a structured (bureaucratic) organization where employees have little interest (or hope) to participate in higher level decisions, or it could be a division with technically capable, trustworthy employees who have no desire to participate in management decision making. Technicians (scientists, engineers, programmers, etc.) in a high-tech enterprise, for instance, may be quite content to be left alone to do their work. Their professional training and peer influence are likely to have given them a "built-in compass" focused on doing a "professional" job. However, in either of these situations, the autocratic leader has to have the depth of expertise needed to make decisions without consulting subordinates.

The Directive Democrat

This type of leader invites full participation from subordinates in decision making. However, he or she still supervises employees very closely to make sure they carry out their democratically assigned tasks properly. A directive democrat would be called for when employee involvement is important to the decision process, such as in a very complex undertaking involving many interdependent activities—a situation where a timely response is less important than a technically correct one. The extensive direction would be needed here if employees lack either experience and ability or reliability and initiative. The directive-democratic combination is also appropriate if the leader is predisposed toward sharing decision making authority but doesn't really trust the reliability of subordinates.

Again, the common interpretation of participation seems to conflict with the idea of close supervision and direction. Yet, this combination may well be the most effective of the four generic leadership behaviors in the vast majority of leadership situations. As pointed out earlier, a great many organizations (business or otherwise) lack the people, systems, or resources needed to support extensive delegation. In these types of organizations leaders must be very directive to make up for any shortages in capabilities and initiative among their subordinates.

An example might be the owner/manager of a small firm who has a strong need to be democratic, but is not fortunate enough to have a highly capable and dependable staff. This situation is all too common among small to medium size firms, which often lack the resources to attract, train, or keep employees capable of extended, independent action. But, it can also be found in larger, bureaucratic organizations that treat employees as expendable, and do not invest in the long-term development of their human resources.

The Permissive Democrat

In a sense, this is the ideal, "All-American" type of leader, since employees get to participate in decision making as well as enjoy a high degree of autonomy in executing the decision. This kind of leader is exemplified by the popular phrase at Texas Instruments: "Every employee a manager." The permissive democrat is suitable for any organization where employee involvement has both informational and motivational benefits. However, this type of leader behavior requires highly qualified employees, some effective substitute(s) for personal direction and enough time to reach consensus. In addition, the leader must value the democratic process and have trust in subordinates' capabilities, judgment, and motives.

The Importance of Leader Direction

The concept of directive leadership has special significance for any organization that lacks the sophisticated structure or systems characteristic of many large, mature institutions. If such a "system-poor" organization also has a high proportion of members who lack self-discipline and initiative, watch out! Here the democratic leader who is also permissive could be downright dangerous. Under such circumstances an absence of leader direction could create serious problems with productivity, goal achievement, and even morale.

While we have found no empirical research that addresses this important issue, practicing management experts are very much aware of it and have even found at least one practical solution. A good example of this is provided by the way some executive recruiters deal with the problem of hiring managers from top notch corporations like IBM. Typically these recruiters will try to avoid placing "pure" IBMers in responsible managerial posts for less resource-rich firms. Instead, they look for IBM "alumni" who have proven their mettle in other organizations without the safety net of their high-quality systems, staff, and corporate culture. That is, executive head hunters consider seasoned, "once-removed" ex-IBMers far more desirable than those whose managerial experience is limited to IBM's unusually supportive environment.

The inescapable reality is that many small and medium-size enterprises have a serious shortage of managers and staff with the kind of expertise and initiative needed for a participative and nondirective leader to be effective.[15] Many larger organizations who have scrimped in the development of their human resources, or have undergone substantial staff reductions, face similar shortages. In these organizations managers are often "Peter-Principled" into positions for which they were insufficiently trained either through formal education or on-the-job experience.[16]

Leaders in large complex organizations are often removed by many levels from the people carrying out critical assignments. In such organizations, the leader's success rides or falls on the quality of subordinates. The excellent organizations can be effective with a minimum of formal controls because of the built-in substitutes for control provided by a highly trained and motivated workforce and a strong corporate culture.[17] But, when democratic leaders don't have the luxury of these types of human resources or of effective control systems, they can't afford to be too permissive. If they delegate authority, they can lose control over end results, unless they also provide close personal direction and follow up on the activities of their subordinates.

Examples abound of business organizations where senior managers have lost control over the actions of key subordinates. However, particularly good examples can be found in what may be the most difficult of all organizations to manage: the U.S. Government. The recent "Irangate" affair serves as a very recent illustration of the way a permissive democrat can get into serious trouble without adequate controls. By most accounts, Ronald Reagan has been one of our most effective presidents. His admirable management style is captured best by his own description: "Surround yourself with the best people you can find, delegate authority, and don't interfere as long as the overall policy you've set is being carried out."[18] Reagan's hands-off style apparently worked extremely well in his first six years in office. It didn't start to unravel until two of his former key aides, Chief of Staff James Baker III and Treasury Secretary Donald Regan, decided to swap jobs. Apparently Reagan had let his past successes lull him into thinking that his highly participative and permissive leader behavior would be effective regardless of who his deputies were.

It now appears that Donald Regan was far less effective as chief of staff than he had been running Merrill Lynch and later the Treasury Department. His efforts to streamline the operation of the White House appear to have isolated his boss from critical sources of information. Reagan's permissiveness, in turn, kept him from doing the kind of follow-up needed to avoid losing control over the actions of his subordinates. Since he also lacked a formal system of controls, the President found out too late about the actions of key subordinates that led up to the Iran-Contra debacle.[19]

The Leadership Cycle

The fundamental changes that most organizations undergo as they grow raises the question of whether any given leadership style or approach can be suitable for an organization throughout its lifetime. A number of researchers have studied the evolution of organizations through various stages of development and concluded that the appropriate leadership style tends to change as well.[20] Many leaders who were successful in one stage find that their styles are no longer effective in the next. A classic example is Ford Motor Company. Henry Ford I by all accounts was a directive autocrat. He continued to lead in his directive and autocratic manner as the company grew in size and complexity well beyond the limits of one man's absolute governance. The result was the near demise of the company. Ironically, the kind of leadership that was instituted to save Ford Motor was similar to the one adopted in the 1920s by its archrival, General Motors, when it reached about the same stage of organizational evolution.[21]

A more recent example of the dynamics of the leadership cycle is provided by the experience of People Express. Don Burr, founder and CEO of this new airline, was an extraordinarily permissive democrat—quite unlike Henry Ford. In fact, he carried his democratic and permissive leadership behavior to its limit by emphasizing autonomous work groups, constant job rotation, salaries tied to profits, and by giving everyone the title of manager. This highly innovative way of organizing was widely praised and was credited with much of the upstart airline's phenomenal success during its entrepreneurial stage.

However, People Express experienced major difficulties in trying to make it through the next stage of growth. Its explosive expansion naturally increased the organization's complexity, but also made it more and more difficult to find and hire the kind of highly motivated and qualified personnel that made its permissive structure work in the first place. It could no longer afford to keep its treasured, highly participative approach to management and be highly permissive at the same time. Unfortunately, management was reluctant to change what was perceived to have been a fundamental factor in the company's earlier success.[22] The inevitable result was a serious deterioration in performance, culminating in heavy losses and the subsequent takeover by Texas Airlines. Frank Lorenzo, People's new boss, is likely to impose far more directive leadership on the airline as it becomes more formalized. Hopefully this direction will still be combined with the kind of employee participation which has been instrumental in People's past success.

The experience of Robert C. Hazard, Jr., a directive autocrat, can serve as still another illustration. As CEO of Best Western International, Inc., Hazard had achieved great success in bringing the nonprofit motel chain from 800 to 2,597 members between 1974 and 1980. Yet his recent resignation as CEO was greeted with "a collective sigh of relief from Best Western's affiliated hotel owners."[23] His leadership style, immensely successful during the fast growth of Best Western's entrepreneurial and growth stages became a liability as the organization matured. Hotel managers, now much more concerned with profitability and independence than with rapid growth, apparently began to fret under their CEO's autocratic and directive leadership. Mr. Hazard moved on to renewed success as the CEO of the more entrepreneurial Quality Inns International, Inc.—a former competitor with great ambitions for rapid growth. In the meantime, Best Western International appeared to be very satisfied with its new CEO, Ronald A. Evans, a permissive democrat who was "highly regarded" by hotel affiliates.

Best Western had become a mature, highly formal organization operated by confident and capable personnel. Its affiliates both wanted, and could afford, a leader who would be a first among equals and would leave day-to-day operations up to them. Therefore, Best Western could successfully make the transition to a more permissive leader. By contrast, Quality Inns had just gone through a period of decline and just barely avoided bankruptcy. Its hotel affiliates were looking for a strong leader to tell them where to go and how to get there. The most critical difference in leadership requirements here was along the directiveness dimension, and Hazard was just the type of "hands-on" manager needed to accomplish Quality Inns' turnaround.

The experience of BankAmerica constitutes another example of an organization in dire straits turning to a directive autocrat for salvation. Former CEO A. W. "Tom" Clausen, a man so unwilling to listen to others that he was routinely described as "the dictator," was rehired as CEO to save the organization when it became the target for a hostile takeover.[24]

Best Western' experience illustrates an extreme case where an autocratic and directive leader was successfully replaced by a democratic and permissive one. However, we feel that this abrupt and extreme type of transition is the exception rather than the rule. The addition of the direction dimension opens up two less direct and less risky paths from the "pure" autocratic and directive behavior in the earlier stages of growth toward the democratic and permissive leadership usually found in more mature and sophisticated organizations. The two paths from directive autocrat to permissive democrat are illustrated in Figure 8.2. The autocrat and directive leader can try to become either more participative or less directive before turning into a permissive democrat. The key to an effective transition in leadership behaviors may be to change only one dimension at a time.

The value of this advice can be dramatized by the experience of a small company making plastic components for industrial goods. This company was actively managed by its autocratic/directive founder until his semi retirement. At that time, the founder's two sons-in-law assumed day-to-day management of operations. Naturally, they were not prepared to spend all of their waking moments in the plant. Yet, whenever anything out of the ordinary occurred in their absence, everything would come to a halt until one of the sons-in-law was found. Whenever they attempted to lead in a permissive manner (they did not share their father-in-law's managerial philosophy), nothing much happened, because the employees had been accustomed for too long to having the founder not only make the decisions but also direct them with regard to the execution of their tasks.

Fig. 8.2. The Leadership Cycle.

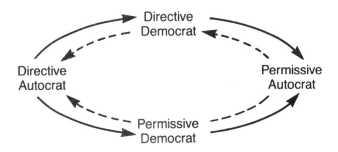

Would it be possible to transform these highly dependent people into more independent ones, capable of being led with a high degree of permissiveness, and all before the firm went bankrupt? Not likely. Still, most employees knew their jobs well and had valuable ideas to offer regarding the improvement of productivity as well as quality. Might not a combination of increased employee participation and very directive leadership be appropriate in this organization, at least for the near term? This would satisfy the new managers' desire for more democratic leadership and take advantage of employee inputs as well. These inputs could make up for the loss of the founder's intimate knowledge of business details and begin to restore a sense of responsibility and initiative among employees. In the meantime, the directive leadership would help to insure that various tasks were accomplished properly and on time.

A successful evolution of leadership behaviors would most frequently take the upper path in Figure 8.2. If, however, a firm with predominantly autocratic and directive leaders succeeds in attracting, developing, and keeping employees that are both capable and independent, its leaders may well be effective by being more permissive. In this case, the evolution toward democratic and permissive leadership may take the lower path in Figure 8.2. This evolution would be the exception rather than the rule, since directive autocrats generally do not do well in attracting, developing, or keeping capable subordinates with high motivation and initiative. One notable exception is provided by the enviable record of the IBM Corporation in its early days. Its founder, Thomas J. Watson, Sr., has been referred to as a dictator. We would call him a directive autocrat. His son and successor, Thomas Watson, Jr., made all the key decisions but allowed subordinates considerable latitude regarding the execution of the decisions. Therefore, we consider his leader behavior to be that of a permissive autocrat. The current top leaders of IBM (Chairman John R. Opel and President and Chief Executive Officer John F. Akers) are clearly permissive democrats—so much so that IBM appears to be run by committees.

Throughout the genesis of IBM, a premium has been placed on sound human relations, high achievement, and rewarding performance. The result has been a strong corporate culture dedicated to quality and the pursuit of excellence by the vast majority of IBM's employees at all levels of the organization. This strong culture gives each loyal employee an internal "gyroscope" that is lined up with the basic goals of the organization, and this provides a powerful substitute for directive leadership. One key to IBM's phenomenal success is the fact that its employees are so firmly committed to its corporate ideals that they need relatively little personal direction or follow-up from their leaders. Without this advantage it is doubtful that an organization as large and complex as IBM could continue to grow and prosper in its rapidly changing environment. The low direction needed at all levels has helped IBM management keep its huge organization highly decentralized yet firmly focused on central corporate goals and values.[25]

In terms of our leadership cycle theory, the transition between Watson, Sr., and his son was reflected primarily in a change in the directive dimension. Both leaders were quite autocratic, but where the founder behaved in a very "hands on" fashion and immersed himself in all the details of the business, his son was unable or unwilling to go to such lengths. Instead the younger Watson decided to delegate responsibilities for individual tasks. On the one hand, the growing size and complexity of the firm made this move necessary, and, on the other, the high quality of IBM's workforce and its strong culture made this increased permissiveness possible. In more recent times, the ever-increasing size and sophistication of the IBM organization and its employees have resulted in a very natural and successful transition toward the ideal leadership combination of high participation and permissiveness.

The leadership cycle shown in Figure 8.2 tends to proceed from left to right, that is, from the directive autocrat toward the permissive democrat. However, the reverse is not unlikely either. A new, entrepreneurial organization is just as likely to be founded and run by a permissive democrat as a directive autocrat (or either of the other two leader types). If so, the cycle may well go from right to left if a more autocratic or directive leader takes over the organization. Sometimes this movement is necessitated by growth or other environmental changes. A fairly common case is that of the democratic and permissive leader whose organization gets itself in trouble—financially, legally, or otherwise. In the Quality Inns case, for example, a tough, hands-on leader like Hazard was needed to turn the company away from the brink of bankruptcy. When the hugely successful Apple Computer began to stumble, its democratic and permissive founder, Stephen Jobs, was replaced by a more directive CEO, former PepsiCo executive John Sculley. Ronald Reagan might have avoided the Irangate-Contra scandal if he had been more directive.

Herbert and Deresky found that even the implementation of different organizational strategies (i.e., develop, stabilize, and turnaround) calls for general managers with different sets of managerial actions, skills, experience, and behaviors. To the extent that organizations need different strategies in different stages of the organizational life cycle, their research lends support to the leadership cycle notions that we have proposed here.[26]

The Real Leadership Challenge

The unbridled enthusiasm for democracy and individual autonomy that pervades the very fiber of our society seems to have blinded many scholars and practitioners to the fact that few organizations can really achieve this ideal state in the workplace. The inescapable fact is that many, many organizations who are less than "excellent" in the caliber of their people and support systems simply can't afford to have their managers be participative without a commensurate dose of direction. That is, in the vast majority of actual leadership situations democratic behaviors must be tempered with a measure of direction or follow-up to assure that organizational goals are accomplished efficiently and effectively.

Actually, the excellent organizations make their leaders' jobs easy—even routine. The real challenge to leadership is posed by those organizations that lack the resources to facilitate extensive participation and delegation. It is in these tough situations that leaders can be of real value. Instead of directing the organization's abundant resources, leaders must themselves act as resources for their followers.

In particular, those managers who want to encourage employee participation must make every effort to guide and develop their subordinates and follow up on their activities. Failure to do so can result in reduced performance for the organization and, therefore, failure for the manager. Like Gerry Gladstone, the participative manager may delegate himself (or herself) right out of a job!

Notes

1. See Henry Mintzberg, *The Nature of Managerial Work* (New York: Harper & Row, 1973).

2. A search of only one of Dialog's databases (File B15: ABI/Inform) resulted in 12,025 listings under "leader?" (which would include such references as "leaders" or "leader behavior") and 5,479 under the full designation of "leadership." While many of these references dealt only indirectly with the subject of leadership, the data base also goes back only to 1971.

3. For a good summary of these major leadership theories, see Gary A. Yukl, *Leadership in Organizations* (Englewood Cliffs, NJ: Prentice-Hall, Inc., 1981).

4. For an excellent discussion about the values and expectations of the generation growing to maturity during the 1960's, and some implications for today's managers, see Joseph A. Raelin, "The 60's Kids in the Corporation: More Than Just 'Daydream Believers,'" the *Academy of Management Executive*, February 1987, pp. 21-30.

5. Perhaps the most influential book extolling the virtues of participative management in major corporations is *In Search of Excellence* by Thomas J. Peters and Robert H. Waterman, Jr., (New York: Harper & Row, 1982.) Also see Terrence E. Deal and Allen A. Kennedy, *Corporate Cultures* (Reading, Mass: Addison-Wesley, 1982) and William G. Ouchi, *Theory Z* (New York: Avon Books, 1981).

6. See Jan P. Muczyk and Bernard C. Reimann, "Has Participative Management Been Oversold?" *Personnel*, May 1987, pp. 52-56.

7. These conflicting results of research on participative management have been well documented by Yukl (Endnote 3) and by E. A. Locke and D. M. Schweiger, "Participation in Decision Making: One More Look," *Research on Organization Behavior*, 1979, pp. 265-339. For a particularly thorough critique of some of the major studies, see Arlyn J. Melcher, "Participation: A Critical Review of Research Findings," *Human Resource Management*, Summer 1976, pp. 12-21.

8. See Robert R. Blake and Jane S. Mouton, *The Managerial Grid* (Houston: Gulf Publishing, 1964).

9. We consider this concern for production variable to be distinct from the Ohio State researchers' "initiating structure" dimension, which deals more explicitly with follow-up or directive behavior. We believe that a permissive leader can be, and often is, high in concern for production through a management by objectives type of approach rather than through frequent follow-up and/or coaching.

10. For the evidence and rationale supporting the importance of creating and maintaining a strong nexus between performance and rewards see the following: Lawler, E. E. "Whatever Happened to Incentive Pay," *New Management*, Vol. 1 (4), 1984, pp. 37-41; Muczyk, J. P., and Hastings, R. E., "In Defense of Enlightened Hardball Management," *Business Horizons*, July/August 1985, pp. 23-29; Muczyk, J. P. "The Strategic Role of Compensation," *Human Resource Planning* (in print).

11. See M. G. Evans, "The Effects of Supervisory Behavior on the Path-Goal Relationship," *Organizational Behavior and Human Performance*, 1970, 5, pp. 277-298, and Robert J. House, "A Path-Goal Theory of Leader Effectiveness," *Administrative Science Quarterly*, 1971, pp. 321-339.

12. Blake and Mouton (Endnote 8) exemplify the normative approach, while Fred Fiedler is best known for his situational theory of leadership. (See his articles, "Engineering the Job to Fit the Manager." *Harvard Business Review*, September-October 1965, pp. 115-122, or "The Leadership Game: Matching the Man to the Situation," *Organizational Dynamics*, Winter 1976, pp. 6-16.)

13. Our situational prescriptions for the four generic leadership behaviors are based on the approach taken by Robert Tannenbaum and Warren Schmidt in their classic article, "How to Choose a Leadership Pattern," *Harvard Business Review*, May/June 1973, pp. 162-80.

14. See Timothy K. Smith and Laura Landro's article, "Coke's Future: Profoundly Changed, Coca-Cola Co. Strives to Keep on Bubbling," *The Wall Street Journal*, April 24, 1986, p. 1.

15. Small and medium-size firms typically do not pay as well as large firms. Also, premature promotions are particularly likely in smaller firms, which typically have four or fewer organizational levels (e.g., employees, supervisors, managers or vice-presidents in charge of functional areas, and presidents). Hence, only two promotions will get you a vice-presidency in a small firm. Also, the smaller the firm, the more limited the choices for a given opening. To make matters worse, many small firms (especially privately held or family-owned ones) are loath to go to the external labor market even if they cannot find a qualified internal candidate. Since the vast majority of business firms are of the small and relatively resource-poor variety, most practicing managers face situations with limited support from ideally qualified subordinates or sophisticated systems.

16. See Carole and Bryant Cushing, "Fitting Managers Into Management," *Financial Executive*, January 1987, .pp. 4-5.

17. See Peters and Waterman or Deal and Kennedy (Endnote 5).

18. For a detailed discussion of Ronald Reagan's leadership and its impact on Irangate, see Ann Reilly Dowd, "Learning from Reagan's Debacle," *Fortune*, April 27, 1987, pp. 169-172.

19. Leader behavior was not the only management failure leading to the Irangate scandal, of course. For a perceptive analysis of the broader management issues, see Peter F. Drucker, "Management Lessons of Irangate," *The Wall Street Journal*, March 1987, p. 32.

20. For some in-depth analyses of organizational life cycles see Larry E. Greiner, "Evolution and Revolution as Organizations Grow," *Harvard Business Review*, July/August 1972, pp. 37-46, and Robert E. Quinn and Kim Cameron, "Organizational Life Cycles and Some Shifting Criteria of Effectiveness: Some Preliminary Evidence," *Management Science*, 1983, pp. 33-51.

21. See Martin J. Gannon, *Management: An Integrated Framework*, 2nd Ed, (Boston, MA: Little, Brown & Co., 1982).

22. See Amanda Bennett, "Airline's Ills Point Out Weaknesses of Unorthodox Management Style," *The Wall Street Journal*, August 11, 1986.

23. See "Matching Managers to a Company's Life Cycle," *Business Week*, February 23, 1981, p. 62. Also, Julie Solomon's "Kroger Says Kagler Quit as President Because of Differences With Chairman," *The Wall Street Journal*, October 28, 1986, p. 42, and "Heirs Apparent to Chief Executives Often Trip Over Prospect of Power," *The Wall Street Journal*, March 24, 1987, p. 35.

24. See Christian G. Hill and Richard. B. Schmitt, "Autocrat Tom Clausen Faces Formidable Task to Save BankAmerica," *The Wall Street Journal*, October 17, 1986, p. 1.

25. Much of the background information about IBM's evolution and management practices was drawn from the following articles in *The Wall Street Journal*, April 7, 1986: "Behind the Monolith: A Look at IBM," by John Marcom, Jr. (p. 15); "IBM, Once a Dictatorship, is Now a Vast Decentralized Democracy," by Randall Smith (p. 16); and "Working at IBM: Intense Loyalty in a Rigid Culture," by Dennis Keale (p. 17).

26. See Theodore T. Herbert and Helen Deresky, "Should General Managers Match Their Business Strategies?" *Organizational Dynamics*, Winter 1987, pp. 40-51.

9
LEADERSHIP: MORE DOING THAN DASH

Peter F. Drucker

Leadership is all the rage just now. "We'd want you to run a seminar for us on how one acquires charisma," the human-resources VP of a big bank said to me on the telephone—in dead earnest. Books, articles and conferences on leadership and on the "qualities" of the leader abound. Every CEO, it seems, has to be made to look like a dashing Confederate cavalry general or a board-room Elvis Presley.

Leadership does matter, of course. But, alas, it is something different from what is now touted under this label. It has little to do with "leadership qualities" and even less to do with "charisma." It is mundane, unromantic and boring. Its essence is performance.

In the first place, leadership is not by itself good or desirable. Leadership is a means. Leadership to what end is thus the crucial question. History knows no more charismatic leaders than this century's triad of Stalin, Hitler and Mao—the misleaders who inflicted as much evil and suffering on humanity as have ever been recorded.

The Undoing of Leaders

But effective leadership doesn't depend on charisma. Dwight Eisenhower, George Marshall and Harry Truman were singularly effective leaders yet none possessed any more charisma than a dead mackerel. Nor did Konrad Adenauer, the chancellor who rebuilt West Germany after World War II. No less charismatic personality could be imagined than Abe Lincoln of Illinois, the raw-boned, uncouth backwoodsman of 1860. And there was amazingly little charisma to the bitter, defeated, almost broken Churchill of the inter-war years; what mattered was that he turned out in the end to have been right.

Reprinted by permission from *The Wall Street Journal*, 69:58 (January 6, 1988), p. 16.

Indeed, charisma becomes the undoing of leaders. It makes them inflexible, convinced of their own infallibility, unable to change. This is what happened to Stalin, Hitler, and Mao, and it is a commonplace in the study of ancient history that only Alexander the Great's early death saved him from becoming an ineffectual failure.

Indeed, charisma does not by itself guarantee effectiveness as a leader. John F. Kennedy may have been the most charismatic person ever to occupy the White House. Yet few presidents got as little done.

Nor are there any such things as "leadership qualities" or a "leadership personality." Franklin D. Roosevelt, Winston Churchill, George Marshall, Dwight Eisenhower, Bernard Montgomery and Douglas MacArthur, were all highly effective—and highly visible—leaders during World War II. No two of them shared any "personality traits" or any "qualities."

What then is leadership if it is not charisma and not a set of personality traits? The first thing to say about it is that it is work—something stressed again and again by the most charismatic leaders: Julius Caesar, for instance, or Gen. MacArthur and Field Marshal Montgomery; or to use an example from business, Alfred Sloan, the man who built and led General Motors from 1920 to 1955.

The foundation of effective leadership is thinking through the organization's mission, defining it and establishing it, clearly and visibly. The leader sets the goals, sets the priorities, and sets and maintains the standards. He makes compromises, of course; indeed, effective leaders are painfully aware that they are not in control of the universe. (Only misleaders—the Stalins, Hitlers, Maos—suffer from that delusion.) But before accepting a compromise, the effective leader has thought through what is right and desirable. The leader's first task is to be the trumpet that sounds a clear sound.

What distinguishes the leader from the misleader are his goals. Whether the compromise he makes with the constraints of reality— which may involve political, economic, financial or people problems— are compatible with his mission and goals or lead away from them determines whether he is an effective leader. And whether he holds fast to a few basic standards (exemplifying them in his own conduct) or whether "standards" for him are what he can get away with, determines whether the leader has followers or only hypocritical timeservers.

The second requirement is that the leader see leadership as responsibility rather than as rank and privilege. Effective leaders are rarely "permissive." But when things go wrong—and they always do—they do not blame others. If Winston Churchill is an example of leadership through clearly defining mission and goals, Gen. George Marshall, America's chief of staff in World War II, is an example of leadership through responsibility. Harry Truman's folksy "The buck stops here" is still as good a definition as any.

But precisely because an effective leader knows that he, and no one else, is ultimately responsible, he is not afraid of strength in associates and subordinates. Misleaders are; they always go in for purges. But an effective leader wants strong associates; he encourages them, pushes them, indeed glories in them. Because he holds himself ultimately responsible for the mistakes of his associates and subordinates, he also sees the triumphs of his associates and subordinates as his triumphs, rather than as threats. A leader may be personally vain—as Gen. MacArthur was to an almost pathological degree. Or he may be personally humble—both Lincoln and Truman were so almost to the point of having inferiority complexes. But all three wanted able, independent, self-assured people around them; they encouraged their associates and subordinates, praising and promoting them. So did a very different person: Ike Eisenhower, when supreme commander in Europe.

An effective leader knows, of course, that there is a risk: Able people tend to be ambitious. But he realizes that it is a much smaller risk than to be served by mediocrity. He also knows that the gravest indictment of a leader is for the organization to collapse as soon as he leaves or dies, as happened in Russia the moment Stalin died and as happens all too often in companies. An effective leader knows that the ultimate task of leadership is to create human energies and human vision.

Earning Trust is a Must

The final requirement of effective leadership is to earn trust. Otherwise there won't be any followers—and the only definition of a leader is someone who has followers. To trust a leader, it is not necessary to like him. Nor is it necessary to agree with him. Trust is the conviction that the leader means what he says. It is a belief in something very old-fashioned, called "integrity." A leader's actions and a leader's professed beliefs must be congruent, or at least compatible. Effective leadership—and again this is very old wisdom—is not based on being clever; it is based primarily on being consistent.

After I had said these things on the telephone to the bank's human-resources VP, there was a long silence. Finally she said: "But that's no different at all from what we have known for years are the requirements for being an effective manager."

Precisely.

10
LEADERSHIP: GOOD, BETTER, BEST

Bernard M. Bass

What does Lee Iacocca have that many other executives lack? Charisma. What would have happened to Chrysler without him? It probably would have gone bankrupt. Here are two more questions: How much does business and industry encourage the emergence of leaders like Iacocca? And how much effort has organizational psychology put into research on charismatic leadership? The answers are that business and industry have usually discouraged charismatic leadership and that, for the most part, organizational psychology has ignored the subject. It has been customary to see leadership as a method of getting subordinates to meet job requirements by handing out rewards or punishments.

Take a look at Barry Bargainer. Barry considers himself to be a good leader. He meets with subordinates to clarify expectations—what is required of them and what they can expect in return. As long as they meet his expectations, Barry doesn't bother them.

Cynthia Changer is a different kind of leader. When facing a crisis, Cynthia inspires her team's involvement and participation in a "mission." She solidifies it with simple words and images and keeps reminding her staff about it. She has frequent one-to-one chats with each of her employees at his or her work station. She is consultant, coach, teacher, and mother figure.

Barry Bargainer, a transactional leader, may inspire a reasonable degree of involvement, loyalty, commitment, and performance from his subordinates. But Cynthia Changer, using a transformational approach, can do much more.

Organizational Dynamics, (1985), pp. 26-40. Reprinted with permission of The Free Press, a Division of Macmillan, Inc., from LEADERSHIP AND PERFORMANCE BEYOND EXPECTATIONS by Bernard M. Bass. Copyright 1985 by The Free Press.

The first part of this article contrasts transactional and transformational leadership styles and the results that are obtained when managers select each approach. The second section reports on surveys of personnel in the military and in industry and examines factors in both approaches to leadership, as they emerged from the survey results. Transformational leadership is presented as a way to augment transactional approaches to management, since it is often more effective in achieving higher levels of improvement and change among employees.

A New Paradigm

For half a century, leadership research has been devoted to studying the effects of democratic and autocratic approaches. Much investigative time has gone into the question of who should decide—the leader or the led. Equally important to research has been the distinction between task orientation and relations orientation. Still another issue has been the need for the leader to "initiate structure" for subordinates and to be considerate of them. At the same time, increasing attention has been paid to the ability to promote change in individuals, groups, and organizations.

The need to promote change and deal with resistance to it has, in turn, put an emphasis on democratic, participative, relations-oriented, and considerate leadership. Contingent rewards have been stressed in training and research with somewhat limited results.

In the past, we have mostly considered how to marginally improve and maintain the quantity or quality of performance, how to substitute one goal for another, how to shift attention from one action to another, how to reduce resistance to particular actions, or how to implement decisions. But higher-order changes are also possible. Increases in effort and the rate at which a group's speed and accuracy improve can sometimes be accelerated. Such higher-order changes also may involve a larger shift in attitudes, beliefs, values, and needs. Quantum leaps in performance may result when a group is roused out of its despair by a leader with innovative or revolutionary ideas and a vision of future possibilities. Leaders may help bring about a radical shift in attention. The context may be changed by leaders. They may change what the followers see as figure and what they see as ground or raise the level of maturity of their needs and wants. For example, followers' concerns may be elevated from their need for safety and security to their need for recognition and achievement.

The lower order of improvement—changes in degree or marginal improvement—can be seen as the result of leadership that is an exchange process: a *transaction* in which followers' needs are met if their performance measures up to their explicit or implicit contracts with their leader. But higher-order improvement calls for *transformational* leadership. There is a great deal of difference between the two types of leadership.

Transactional Leadership in Action

Transactional leaders like Barry Bargainer recognize what actions subordinates must take to achieve outcomes. Transactional leaders clarify these role and task requirements for their subordinates so that they are confident in exerting necessary efforts. Transactional leaders also recognize subordinates' needs and wants and clarify how they will be satisfied if necessary efforts are made. (See Figure 10.1) This approach is currently stressed in leadership training, and it is good as far as it goes; however, the transactional approach has numerous shortcomings.

First, even after training, managers do not fully utilize transactional leadership. Time pressures, poor appraisal methods, doubts about the efficacy of positive reinforcement, leader and subordinate discomfort with the method, and lack of management skills are all partly responsible. How reinforcements are scheduled, how timely they are, and how variable or consistent they are all mediate the degree of their influence.

Some leaders, practicing management by exception, intervene only when things go wrong. In this instance, the manager's discomfort about giving negative feedback is even more self-defeating. When supervisors attribute poor performance to lack of ability, they tend to "pull their punches" by distorting feedback so that it is more positive than it should be.

Another common problem occurs when supervisors say and actually believe they are giving feedback to their subordinates, who feel they are not receiving it. For example, Barry Bargainer may meet with his group of subordinates to complain that things are not going well. Barry thinks he is giving negative feedback while his subordinates only hear Barry grumbling about conditions. Barry may give Henry a pat on the back for a job he thinks has been well done. Henry may feel that he knows he did a good job, and it was condescending for Barry to mention it.

People differ considerably in their preference for external reinforcement or self-reinforcement. Task-oriented and experienced subordinates generally are likely to be self-reinforcing. They may say: "If I have done something well, I know it without other people telling me so," and "As long as I think that I have done something well, I am not too concerned about what other people think I have done."

Fig. 10.1. Transactional Leadership (L = Leaders; F = Followers)

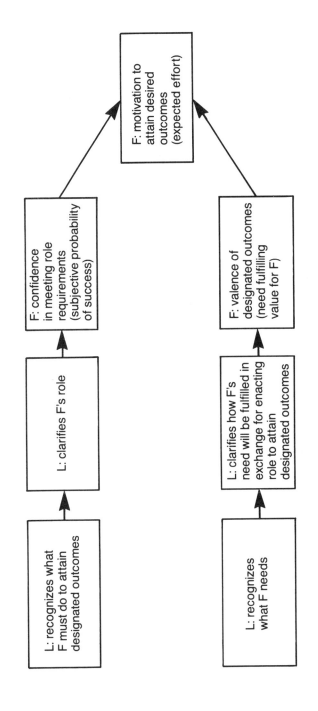

Subordinates and supervisors attach differing importance to various kinds of feedback. Many subordinates attach more importance than do supervisors to their own success or failure with particular tasks, and to their own comparisons with the work of others. Subordinates are also likely to attach more importance than do supervisors to co-workers' comments about their work. Supervisors tend to put the most weight on their own comments to their subordinates, and to recommendations for rewards they, as supervisors, can make, such as raises, promotions, and more interesting assignments.

Transactional leadership often fails because the leaders lack the reputation for being able to deliver rewards. Transactional leaders who fulfill the self-interested expectations of their subordinates gain and maintain the reputation for being able to deliver pay, promotions, and recognition. Those that fail to deliver lose their reputation and are not considered to be effective leaders.

Transactional leadership may be abandoned by managers when noncontingent rewards (employees are treated well, regardless of performance) will work just as well to boost performance. For example, in a large nonprofit organization, a study by Phillip Podsakoff et al. showed that contingent rewards (those given only if performance warrants them) did contribute to employee performance, but noncontingent rewards were correlated almost as strongly with performance as contingent rewards.

Noncontingent rewards may provide a secure situation in which employees' self-reinforcement serves as a consequence for good performance (for example, IBM's straight salaries for all employees). An employee's feeling of obligation to the organization for providing noncontingent rewards fuels his or her effort to perform at least adequately. The Japanese experience is exemplary; in the top third of such Japanese firms as Toyota, Sony, and Mitsubishi, employees and the companies feel a mutual sense of life-time obligation. Being a good family member does not bring immediate pay raises and promotions, but overall family success will bring year-end bonuses. Ultimately, opportunities to advance to a higher level and salary will depend on overall meritorious performance.

When the contingent reinforcement used is aversive (reinforcement that recipients prefer to avoid), the success of the transactional leader usually plummets. In the same not-for-profit organization studied by Podsakoff et al., neither contingent reprimand, disapproval, nor punishment had any effect on performance or overall employee satisfaction. The same results have been observed in other organizations. Contingent approval and disapproval by results-oriented leaders did improve subordinates' understanding of what was expected of them but failed to have much effect on motivation or performance. In general, reprimand may be useful in highlighting what not to do, but usually it does not contribute to positive motivation, particularly when subordinates are expected to be innovative and creative.

Even when it is based solely on rewards, transactional leadership can have unintended consequences. When expounding on the principles of leadership, Vice Admiral James B. Stockdale argued that people do not like to be programmed:

> . . . You cannot persuade (people) to act in their own self-interest all of the time. A good leader appreciates contrariness.

> . . . Some men all of the time and all men some of the time knowingly will do what is clearly to their disadvantage if only because they do not like to be suffocated by carrot-and-stick coercion. I will not be a piano key; I will not bow to the tyranny of reason.

In working subtly against transactional leadership, employees may take short-cuts to complete the exchange of reward for compliance. For instance, quality may suffer if the leader does not monitor it as closely as he or she does the quantity of output. The employee may begin to react defensively rather than adequately; in some cases, reaction formation, withdrawal, hostility, or "game playing" may result.

The Alternative: Add Transformational Leadership to the Manager-Employee Relationship

James McGregor Burns, the biographer of Franklin D. Roosevelt and of John F. Kennedy, was the first to contrast transactional with transformational leadership. The transformational leader motivates us to do more than we originally expected to do. Such a transformation can be achieved in the following ways:

1. Raising our level of consciousness about the importance and value of designated outcomes and ways of reaching these outcomes.
2. Getting us to transcend our own self-interests for the sake of the team, organization, or larger polity.
3. Raising our need level on Abraham Maslow's hierarchy from, say, the need for security to the need for recognition, or expanding our portfolio of needs by, for example, adding the need for self-actualization to the need for recognition.

Cynthia Changer is a transformational leader; Barry Bargainer is not. Figure 10.2 is a model of transformational leadership that starts with a current level of effort based on a follower's current level of confidence and desire for designated outcomes. A transactional leader contributes to such confidence and desire by clarifying what performance is required and how needs will be satisfied as a consequence. The transformational leader induces additional effort by directly increasing the follower's confidence as well as by elevating the value of outcomes through expanding his or her transcendental interests and level or breadth of needs in Maslow's hierarchy.

The need for more transformational leaders in business and industry was illustrated in an in-depth interview survey of a representative national sample of 845 working Americans. The survey found that while most employees liked and respected their managers, they felt their managers really didn't know how to motivate employees to do their best. Although 70% endorsed the work ethic, only 23% said they were working as hard as they could in their jobs. Only 9% agreed that their performance was motivated by transaction; most reported that there actually was little connection between how much they earned and the level of effort they put into the job.

Report on a Study of Transformational Leadership

I set out to find evidence of transformational leadership and its effects at various levels in industrial and military organizations, *not just at the top.*

I defined transformational leadership for 70 senior executives. Then, I asked them to describe in detail a transformational leader whom they had encountered at any time during their career. All respondents claimed to have known at least one such person. Most cited a former immediate supervisor or higher-level manager in the organization. A few mentioned family members, consultants, or counselors.

This transformational leader induced respondents to work ridiculous hours *and to do more than they ever expected to do.* Respondents reported that they aimed to satisfy the transformational leader's expectations and to give the leader all the support asked of them. They wanted to emulate the leader. The transformational leader increased their awareness of and promoted a higher quality of performance and greater innovativeness. Such a leader convinced followers to extend themselves and to develop themselves further. Total commitment to and belief in the organization emerged as consequences of belief in the leader and heightened self-confidence.

Many respondents (all were male) indicated that the transformational leader they could identify in their own careers was like a benevolent father who remained friendly and treated the respondent as an

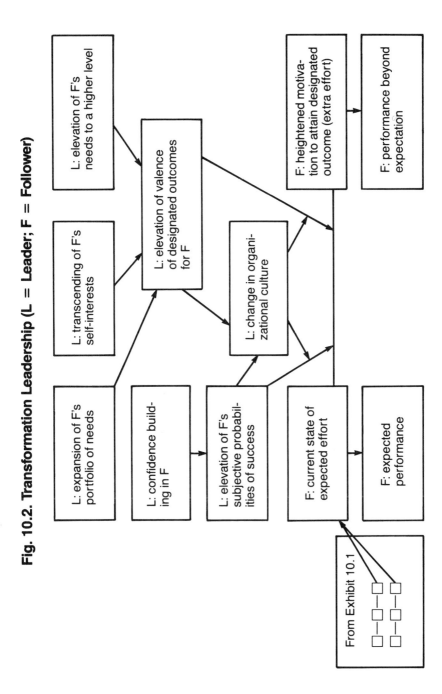

Fig. 10.2. Transformation Leadership (L = Leader; F = Follower)

equal despite the leader's greater knowledge and experience. The leader provided a model of integrity and fairness and also set clear and high standards of performance. He encouraged followers with advice, help, support, recognition, and openness. He gave followers a sense of confidence in his intellect, yet was a good listener. He gave followers autonomy and encouraged their self-development. He was willing to share his greater knowledge and expertise with them. Yet he could be formal and firm and would reprimand followers when necessary. Most respondents, however, were inclined to see the transforming leader as informal and accessible. Such a leader would be counted on to stand up for his subordinates. Along with the heightened and changed motivation and awareness, frequent reactions of followers to the transforming leader included trust, strong liking, admiration, loyalty, and respect.

In conducting a second survey, I used the descriptions from the first to create a questionnaire of 73 behavioral items. Responses to each item were on a five-point frequency scale. A total of 176 senior U.S. Army officers completed the questionnaire describing the behavior of their immediate superiors. Five factors emerged from a statistical factor analysis of the data. Two dealt with transactional leadership, the exchange relationship between superior and subordinate: contingent reward, by which subordinates earned benefits for compliance with the leader's clarification of the paths toward goals, and management by exception, by which the leader gave negative feedback for failure to meet agreed-upon standards. Three of the factors dealt with transformational leadership—the broadening and elevating of goals and of subordinates' confidence in their ability to go beyond expectations. These factors were (1) charismatic leadership (leaders aroused enthusiasm, faith, loyalty, and pride and trust in themselves and their aims); (2) individualized consideration (leaders maintained a developmental and individualistic orientation toward subordinates); and (3) intellectual stimulation (leaders enhanced the problem-solving capabilities of their associates). An interesting sidelight was that more transformational leadership was observed (by respondents) in combat units than in support units.

As expected, the three transformational factors were more highly correlated with perceived unit effectiveness than were the two transactional factors. Parallel results were obtained for subordinates' satisfaction with their leader. Charismatic, considerate, and intellectually stimulating leaders were far more satisfying to work for than were those who merely practiced the transactions of contingent reinforcement. I obtained similar results from a survey of 256 business managers, 23 educational administrators, and 45 professionals. Moreover, in these latter samples, respondents reported that they made greater efforts when leaders were charismatic, individualizing, and intellectually stimulating. Contingent reward was also fairly predictive of extra effort, but management by exception was counterproductive. Further analysis of the data by my colleague, David Waldman, supported the model shown in Figure 10.2. The analysis demonstrated that when a leader displayed transformational abilities and engaged in transactional relationships, extra effort made by subordinates was above and beyond what could be attributed to transactional factors alone.

Transactional Factors: Contingent Reinforcement and Management by Exception

According to our questionnaire surveys, positive and aversive contingent reinforcement are the two ways managers in organized settings engage in transactional leadership to influence employee performance. Ordinarily, contingent reward takes two forms: praise for work well done and recommendations for pay increases, bonuses, and promotion. In addition, this kind of reward can take the form of commendations for effort or public recognition and honors for outstanding service.

Contingent punishment can take several forms as a reaction to a deviation from norms—when, for example, production falls below agreed-upon standards or quality falls below acceptable levels. The manager may merely call attention to the deviation. Being told of one's failure to meet standards may be sufficient punishment to change behavior. Being told why one has failed can be helpful, particularly to the inexperienced or inexpert subordinate, especially if the negative feedback is coupled with further clarification about what kind of performance is expected. While other penalties—such as fines, suspensions without pay, loss of leader support, or discharge—may be imposed, these are less frequently used and less likely to promote effectiveness.

When the manager, for one reason or another, chooses to intervene only when failures, breakdowns, and deviations occur, he or she is practicing management by exception. The rationale of those who use this practice is, "If it ain't broke, don't fix it!" The research studies I have completed with military officers, business executives, professionals, and educational administrators generally indicate that as a steady diet, management by exception can be counterproductive. But contingent rewards yield a fairly good return in terms of subordinate effort and performance. Nevertheless, in the aggregate, there will be additional payoff when the transformational factors appear in a leader's portfolio.

Charismatic and Inspirational Leadership

Charisma is not exclusively the province of world-class leaders or a few generals or admirals. It is to be found to some degree in industrial and military leaders throughout organizations. Furthermore, charisma is the most important component in the larger concept of transformational leadership. In my study I found that many followers described their military or industrial leader as someone who made everyone enthusiastic about assignments, who inspired loyalty to the organization, who commanded respect from everyone, who had a special gift of seeing what was really important, and who had a sense or mission that excited responses. Followers had complete faith in the leaders with charisma, felt proud to be associated with them, and trusted their capacity to overcome any obstacle. Charismatic leaders served as symbols of success and accomplishment for their followers.

Charisma is one of the elements separating the ordinary manager from the true leader in organizational settings. The leader attracts intense feeling of love (and sometimes hatred) from his or her subordinates. They want to identify with the leader. Although feelings about ordinary managers are bland, relations are smoother and steadier. Like most intimate relationships, the relations between the charismatic leader and his or her followers tend to be more turbulent.

There may be a scarcity of charismatic leaders in business and industry because managers lack the necessary skills. On the other hand, managers who have the skills may not recognize the opportunity or may be unwilling to risk what is required to stand out so visibly among their peers. More charismatic leaders potentially exist in organizational settings; furthermore, they may be necessary to an organization's success.

The ability to inspire—arouse emotions, animate, enliven, or even exalt—is an important aspect of charisma. Inspirational leadership involves the arousal and heightening of motivation among followers. Followers can be inspired by a cold, calculating, intellectual discourse, the brilliance of a breakthrough, or the beauty of an argument. Yet it is the followers' emotions that ultimately have been aroused. Followers may hold an intellectual genius in awe and reverence, but the inspirational influence on them is emotional.

Consider the specific leadership behaviors Gary Yukl used to illustrate what he meant by inspirational leadership:

> My supervisor held a meeting to talk about how vital the new contract is for the company and said he was confident we could handle it if we all did our part. My boss told us we were the best design group he had ever worked with and he was sure that this new product was going to break every sales record in the company.

The inspiring supervisor was not dispassionate. The supervisor talked about how *vital* the new contract was to the company. He said he was *confident* in his people. He told them they were the *best* group he had *ever* worked with. He was sure the product would *break every record*.

In summary, as a consequence of his or her self-confidence, absence of inner conflict, self-determination, and requisite abilities, a leader will be held in high esteem by followers, particularly in times of trouble. He or she can generally inspire them by emotional support and appeals that will transform their level of motivation beyond original expectations. Such a leader can sometimes also inspire followers by means of intellectual stimulation. The charismatic leader can do one or the other, or both.

Individualized Consideration

The transformational leader has a developmental orientation toward followers. He evaluates followers' potential both to perform their present job and to hold future positions of greater responsibility. The leader sets examples and assigns tasks on an individual basis to followers to help significantly alter their abilities and motivations as well as to satisfy immediate organizational needs.

Delegating challenging work and increasing subordinate responsibilities are particularly useful approaches to individualized development. As General Omar Bradley pointed out, there is no better way to develop leadership than to give an individual a job involving responsibility and let him work it out. A survey of 208 chief executives and senior officers by Charles Margerison reported that important career influences on them before age 35 included being "stretched" by immediate bosses and being given leadership experience, overall responsibility for important tasks, and wide experience in many functions.

The transformational leader will consciously or unconsciously serve as a role model for subordinates. For example, in the Margerison survey, the executives attributed their own successful development as managers to having had early on in their careers managers who were models.

Managerial training supports the idea that managers profit from role models. What may be different in what I propose, however, is that the transformational leader emphasizes *individualism*. Personal influence and the one-to-one superior-subordinate relationship is of primary importance to the development of leaders. An organizational culture of individualism, even of elitism, should be encouraged; an organization should focus attention on identifying prospective leaders among subordinates.

Individualized attention is viewed as especially important by the new military commander of a unit. The commander is expected to learn the names of all those in the units at least two levels below his and to become familiar with their jobs. *Military leaders need to avoid treating all subordinates alike.* They must discover what best motivates each individual soldier or sailor and how to employ him most effectively. They must be generous in the use of their time. But as General Eugene Meyer notes, the leaders' interest must be genuine.

Individualized consideration implies that seniors maintain face-to-face contact or at least frequent telephone contact with juniors. The Intel Corporation accepted the fact that recently graduated engineers are more up-to-date on the latest advances in technology than are experienced executives of greater power and status in the firm. Therefore, the firm has consciously encouraged frequent contact and open communication between the recent college graduates and the senior executives through leveling arrangements. Senior executive and junior professionals are all housed in small, unpretentious, accessible offices that share common facilities. The organization stresses that influence is based on knowledge rather than power. In other well-managed firms, "walk-around management" promotes individual contact and communication between those low and high in the hierarchy.

In another study of a high-tech company, Rudi Klauss and Bernard Bass found that project engineers were most influenced by and gained most of their information relevant to decision making from informal contact and individual discussion rather than from written documentation. This company did not believe that the aggregated data from management information systems were the most important inputs for decision making. Rather, two-thirds to three-quarters of the total work time of managers was spent in oral communication. It was the immediate, timely tidbits of gossip, speculation, opinion, and relevant facts that were most influential, not generalized reports reviewing conditions over a recent period of time. Individualized attention of superior to subordinate provided this opportunity for inputs of current and timely information.

Managers are most likely to make face-to-face contact with colleagues at their same organizational level (or by telephone for such colleagues at a distance physically). For superiors and subordinates, written memos are more frequently used. Yet regular, face-to-face debriefing sessions to disseminate important information from superior to subordinate will provide a better basis for organizational decision making and make the superior better equipped to deal with the erratic flow of work and demands on his or her time and the speed that decision making often requires. Unfortunately, unless personal contact becomes a matter of policy (such as walk-around management), communications from superior to subordinate are more likely to be on paper—or now, no doubt, increasingly on computer—rather than face-to-face.

Individualized consideration is reflected when a manager keeps each employee fully informed about what is happening and why—preferably in a two-way conversation rather than a written memo. Employees come to feel that they are on the inside of developments and do not remain bystanders. Sudden changes of plan are less likely to surprise them. If the interaction is two-way, employees have the opportunity to ask questions to clarify understanding. At the same time, managers learn first-hand their subordinates' concerns.

Individualized consideration is also demonstrated when the senior executive or professional takes time to serve as mentor for the junior executive or professional. A mentor is a trusted counselor who accepts a guiding role in the development of a younger or less experienced member of the organization. The mentor uses his or her greater knowledge, experience, and status to help develop his or her protégé and not simply to pull the protégé up the organization ladder on the mentor's coattails. This relationship is different from one in which a manager is supportive or provides advice when asked for it. Compared with the formal, distant relationship most often seen between a high-level executive and a junior somewhere down the line, the mentor is paternalistic or maternalistic and perhaps is a role model for the junior person.

A follow-up of 122 recently promoted people in business indicated that two-thirds had had mentors. This popularity of mentoring in business, government, and industry reflects the current interest on the part of both individuals and organizations in the career development of the individual employee.

Intellectual Stimulation

The statement, "These ideas have forced me to rethink some of my own ideas, which I had never questioned before," sums up the kind of intellectual stimulation that a transformational leader can provide. Intellectual stimulation can lead to other comments like, "She enables me to think about old problems in new ways," or "He provides me with new ways of looking at things that used to be a puzzle for me."

Intellectual stimulation arouses in followers the awareness of problems and how they may be solved. It promotes the hygiene of logic that is compelling and convincing. It stirs the imagination and generates thoughts and insights. It is not the call to immediate action aroused by emotional stimulation. This intellectual stimulation is seen in a discrete leap in the followers' conceptualization, comprehension, and discernment of the nature of the problems they face and their solutions.

Executives should and can play a role as transforming leaders to the degree that they articulate what they discern, comprehend, visualize, and conceptualize to their colleagues and followers. They should articulate what they see as the opportunities and threats facing their organization (or unit within it) and the organization's strengths, weaknesses, and comparative advantages. Leadership in complex organizations must include the ability to manage the problem-solving process in such a way that important problems are identified and solutions of high quality are found and carried out with the full commitment of organization members.

The intellectual component may be obscured by surface considerations. Accused of making snap decisions, General George Patton commented: "I've been studying the art of war for 40-odd years. . . . [A] surgeon who decides in the course of an operation to change its objective is not making a snap decision but one based on knowledge, experience, and training. So am I."

The importance of a leader's technical expertise and intellectual power, particularly in high-performing systems, often is ignored in comparison with the attention paid to his or her interpersonal competence. Where would Polaroid be without Edwin Land? What kind of corporation would Occidental Petroleum be without Armand Hammer?

In this intellectual sphere, we see systematic differences between transformational and transactional leaders. The transformational leader may be less willing to accept the status quo and more likely to seek new ways of doing things while taking maximum advantage of opportunities. Transactional managers will focus on what can clearly work, will keep time constraints in mind, and will do what seems to be most efficient and free of risk.

What may intellectually separate the two kinds of leaders is that transformational leaders are likely to be more proactive than reactive in their thinking, more creative, novel, and innovative in their ideas, and less inhibited in their ideational search for solutions. Transactional leaders may be equally bright, but their focus is on how best to keep running the system for which they are responsible; they react to problems generated by observed deviances and modify conditions as needed while remaining ever mindful of organization constraints.

Transformational Leadership: Benevolent or Malevolent?

Charismatic leadership, individualized consideration, and intellectual stimulation have been clearly seen in the moving and shaking that took place between 1982 and 1984 in a number of firms, such as General Electric, Campbell Soup, and Coca Cola. In each instance, the transformation could be attributed to a newly appointed chief. These transformational leaders were responsible for iconoclastic changes of image, increased organizational flexibility, and an upsurge of new products and new approaches. In each case, the transformational leadership of John F. Welch, Jr., of General Electric, Gordon McGovern of Campbell Soup, and Roberto Goizueta of Coca Cola paid off in invigoration and revitalization of their firms and an acceleration in business success. Clearly, heads may be broken, feelings hurt, and anxieties raised with the advent of transformational leaders such as Welch, McGovern, or Goizueta. "Business as usual" is no longer tolerated. Such transformations may be moral or immoral.

For James Burns, transformational leadership is moral if it deals with true needs and is based on informed choice. The moral transformational leader is one who is guided by such universal ethical principles as respect for human dignity and equal rights. The leadership mobilizes and directs support for "more general and comprehensive values that express followers' more fundamental and enduring needs" (*Leadership*, Harper, 1978). Moral leadership helps followers to see the real conflict between competing values, the inconsistencies between espoused values and behavior, the need for realignments in values, and the need for changes in behavior or transformations of institutions. Burns argued that if the need levels elevated by transformational leaders were not authentic, then the leadership was immoral.

The well-being of organizational life will be better served in the long run by moral leadership. That is, transformations that result in the fulfillment of real needs will prove to be more beneficial to the organization than transformations that deal with manufactured needs and group delusions. Organizational leaders should subscribe to a code of ethics that is accepted by their society and their profession.

The ethical transformational leader aims toward and succeeds in promoting changes in a firm—changes that strengthen firm viability, increase satisfaction of owners, managers, employees, and customers, and increase the value of the firm's products. But transformational leaders can be immoral if they create changes based on false images that cater to the fantasies of constituencies. Firms can be driven into the ground by such leaders. A transformational leader can lull employees and shareholders alike with false hopes and expectations while he or she is preparing to depart in a golden parachute after selling out the company's interests.

Whether transformational or transactional leadership will take hold within an organization will depend to some extent on what is happening or has happened outside of it. Welch, McGovern,and Goizueta all came into power to transform firms that were in danger of failing to keep pace with changes in the marketplace. Transformational leadership is more likely to emerge in times of distress and rapid change.

The personalities of followers will affect a leader's ability to be transformational. Charisma is a two-way process. A leader is seen as charismatic if he or she has followers who imbue him or her with extraordinary value and personal power. This is more easily done when subordinates have highly dependent personalities. On the other hand, subordinates who pride themselves on their own rationality, skepticism, independence, and concern for rules of law and precedent are less likely to be influenced by a charismatic leader or the leader who tries to use emotional inspiration. Subordinates who are egalitarian, self-confident, highly educated, self-reinforcing, and high in status are likely to resist charismatic leaders.

Which Kind of Leadership Should Managers Use?

Managers need to appreciate what kind of leadership is expected of them. Current leadership training and management development emphasize transactional leadership, which is good as far as it goes, but clearly has its limits. Transactional leaders will let their subordinates know what is expected of them and what they can hope to receive in exchange for fulfilling expectations. Clarification makes subordinates confident that they can fulfill expectations and achieve mutually valued outcomes. But subordinates' confidence and the value they place on potential outcomes can be further increased, through transformational leadership. Leadership, in other words, can become an inspiration to make extraordinary efforts.

Charismatic leadership is central to the transformational leadership process. Charismatic leaders have great referent power and influence. Followers want to identify with them and to emulate them. Followers develop intense feelings about them, and above all have trust and confidence in them. Transformational leaders may arouse their followers emotionally and inspire them to extra effort and greater accomplishment. As subordinates become competent with the mainly transformational leader's encouragement and support, contingent reinforcement may be abandoned in favor of self-reinforcement.

Clearly, there are situations in which the transformational approach may not be appropriate. At the same time, organizations need to draw more on the resources of charismatic leaders, who often can induce followers to aspire to and maintain much higher levels of productivity than they would have reached if they had been operating only through the transactional process.

11
DANCING ON
THE GLASS CEILING

Regina E. Herzlinger

At age 43, waiting in a long ladies' room line during a break in a business meeting was a new experience; I usually had the room to myself. Now, here I was at the Financial Accounting Standards Board, jubilantly lining up behind fellow members of an FASB task force on accounting for post-employment benefits other than pensions. All the FASB experts on this arcane subject were women, as were 30% of those representing business, accounting and academia. In 1986, 40% of all accountants and auditors in the U.S. were women, up from virtually none 20 years ago.

The wait in the FASB ladies' room line capped some recent experiences that convinced me that the "glass ceiling" that supposedly keeps women from rising above a certain level in corporations because they are women is a lot of baloney. So, too, is the extensive "documentation" of the especially unhappy lives of young women executives.

Just the week before, I met Potomac Edison's top ranks of middle management engineers, system analysts, line supervisors and construction crews, at least half of whom were female. The week before that, at Bowdoin College's board meeting, nearly all of the committee chairmen were chairwomen, a feat all the more remarkable in a college that first became co-educational in 1970. And the week before that, I lectured to a packed audience of women entrepreneurs at New York's Lincoln Center. These women were accomplished, authoritative, attractive; they weren't craning their necks looking through a "glass ceiling." As Lionel Richie puts it in his song, they were "dancing on the ceiling," savoring a life filled with opportunities never before offered to women.

Reprinted by permission from *The Wall Street Journal*, 69:87 (February 17, 1988), p. 22.

Engineers and Entrepreneurs
Further support for my conviction comes from more impersonal data:

- In 1986, 30% of managers, 16% of lawyers, 20% of doctors and 40% of programmers were female.
- In 1986, 83% of the female officers in the Fortune and Service 500 were at vice presidential or above levels, up from 35% in 1980.
- In 1986, 33% of the people receiving MBAs and 14% receiving engineering degrees were female, vs. 2% in 1966.
- In 1984, 3.5 million self-employed women owned 2.8 million firms. This represented 28% of all U.S. companies, up from 7% in 1977. And the number of female entrepreneurs was growing an average of 9.4% annually, twice the rate of their male counterparts.

Of course, prejudices linger, but the common evocations of bitter—and, worse, unsuccessful—women managers are wrong, emanating from the following five sources of misinformation.

1. *False Prophets*: Women are great readers and even better book buyers, devouring schlock about women—from gothic romances to "Dress for Success." They are also highly responsive to suggestions for self-help and therefore susceptible to a huge industry of false prophets—writers, journalists, aerobics instructors, lecturers, and nutritionists—that encourages and depends on nurturing women's unwarranted sense of failure.

   The scientific branch of false prophecy is false biology, which differentiates the so-called innate managerial capabilities of the sexes: Women are more nurturing (read "soft") and less aggressive (read "weak") than men. Genetic differences are seen as holding women back or, conversely, as the basis for a brave new— future—world of caring management. But until gene mappers find a ruthless gene that is uniquely male and a compassionate gene that is uniquely female, I remain unconvinced that differences in managerial behavior are caused by anything other than differences in social roles.

2. *False Arithmetic*: Simple arithmetic shows that the production of one 1987-vintage female chief executive officer requires thousands of women to have committed themselves to that goal in the college class of 1952, because it takes an average of 35 post-college years to become a CEO. Since most women in 1952 were thinking about the initials MRS., not CEO, it is not surprising that we are not, as yet, deluged by female chief executives.

   When I started teaching at Harvard Business School in 1972, women were about 2% of the MBA class. By 1976, 15% of Harvard

MBA degrees went to women. Using good arithmetic, by 1997 there will be 20 to 30 female big-company CEOs. By 2011, we will see the deluge.

3. *False Failures*: The "glass ceiling" myth rests squarely on the asserted absence of any female Fortune 500 CEOs. But, in reality, there are three female CEOs of Fortune 500 companies, and one of a closely held company that size—Estee Lauder. (If the list is expanded to those billion-dollar utilities and financial institutions not included among the 500, the number increases to eight.) Yet, this extraordinary success is deemed a failure, and the extraordinary accomplishments of the female CEOs are denigrated: Katharine Graham's family owned the Washington Post; Estee Lauder and Liz Claiborne are in traditional women's businesses; and Linda Wachner heads Warnaco, a "lesser known" company.

Geraldine Ferraro is a vivid example of false failure. Although failure is a much more common state than success, the failures of women, particularly the "first" women, are magnified and exaggerated. Ms. Ferraro should be much more notable for her many successes than her failure to attain an exceedingly difficult goal.

4. *False Expectations*: Does every senior executive expect to become a CEO? There is, after all, only one CEO, and because it is a nice job, the turnover is low. Is the female senior manager's glass half-empty or half-full? In 1986, it was more than half-full: The typical female officer of a Fortune and Service 500 firm earned $117,000 a year, was married, and would not have stayed home even if given the same salary to do so.

Equally false is the expectation that younger managers should be happy. Findings of dissatisfaction by younger, female corporate managers misspecify the cause, attributing it to sex, rather than a low organization level that makes men unhappy as well.

5. *False History*: Some point to the failure of the 19th century woman textile worker, the suffragette, the Bloomer Girl, Rosie the Riveter and that Cosmo Girl to become the first female Fortune 500 CEO as verification of the unlikely future progress of women in management. But times really have changed. U.S. companies have become truly multicultural—accepting all kinds of people, as long as they are talented and productive.

Heavy Costs

I don't wish to end this essay with a declaration of victory. The remarkable and wonderful progress of women in corporations has exacted heavy costs and continues to do so, particularly on children. A 1987 survey in Adweek of female advertising executives found that more than half their employers provide no child-care assistance. A third of the respondents said they would readily switch from their present employer to one offering some child-care support. Further, although MIT found its male and female MBAs in the classes of 1974-79 had equal incomes five years after graduation, the pay gap between men and women in other occupations is large, persistent, and inequitable.

Another lingering problem is that the progress of women managers has not been accompanied by a set of comfortable, acceptable images of the new male-female work relationship. Many men and women are therefore unnecessarily awkward and inefficient in working together. For example, a male mentor typically will go out of his way to explain that he has a good working relationship with a protégée and that the relationship is not sexual.

I hope we will overcome these problems so men and women can work together gracefully and share in this rich life. Then we can all dance on the ceiling.

12
QUALITIES OF A SUCCESSFUL CEO

Thomas R. Horton

Becoming a CEO is like becoming a parent. There is no guidebook or training program that provides definitive answers. Chief executive officers must, therefore, find their own ways of fulfilling the multiple responsibilities and roles that are a part of their job.

A specialist in management succession estimates that, based on their performance, one third of incumbent CEOs would not be selected again. However, two thirds were judged effective.

What personal approaches make these CEOs successful? Are they special people who reach the top because of their unique leadership qualities? Or do they go through some magical metamorphosis once they get there? When I interviewed sixteen successful chief executives for my book, *What Works for Me*, we did not talk about their managerial competencies, the actual skills which enable them to do their jobs. Instead, we discussed *qualities*, the inherent characteristics that enable them to *succeed*. What emerged were six qualities shared by these world-class CEOs: their perception of reality, team-building skills, decisiveness, strategic focus, tenacity, and integrity.

Perception of Reality

The successful chief executive has a remarkably sure grasp of what is happening and its significance. The ability to acquire information continuously and select what is relevant is an essential skill.

The chief executive draws heavily. on information networks—both internal and external—and acts as an information processor. However, this is no mechanical process, for there are times when "feeling" is as important as "knowing"; both contribute to a clear perception of reality. As information processors, successful chief executives have highly

Reprinted by permission from *Hyatt Magazine* (Fall 1987), pp. 22-27.

developed sensors. They do not await information but pursue it relentlessly. Bad news is sought with more vigor than good news, for it must be known early enough to do something about it. This input-seeking mechanism is unflinching, reaching out for uncensored, uncolored accounts of events.

What can happen when vital information does not reach the top is starkly illustrated by the Challenger shuttle explosion in early 1986. It was reported during the investigative hearings that although there was a serious conflict at lower levels over the feasibility of a launch on January 28, top-level NASA officials who had to make the ultimate decision learned about the conflict only after the disaster. One also wonders to what degree the lack of essential information at the top contributed to the failures of the unmanned Air Force Titan and NASA Delta rockets a few months after the Challenger disaster—and to the misjudgment blamed by the Russians for the nuclear accident in Chernobyl.

Despite the prodigious amounts of data which arrive at the CEO's desk, there is an unquenchable thirst for more. The volume and firehose velocity of this information flow would overwhelm most executives, but the successful chief develops the capacity to stand to the side, sampling chunks of data as they rush by, looking for patterns and incongruities. To draw meaning from a mass of data in motion requires a capacity to synthesize—an ability to convert data into information and information into knowledge.

In listening to CEOs discuss their important insights, I was struck by their use of anatomical terms such as "a gut-level belief." I once heard an exchange about a complex issue between Thomas G. Watson, Jr., then chairman of IBM, and his executive assistant. Watson asked, "Just on what basis did you reach that decision?" The assistant replied, "Well, in the final analysis, I guess it was a visceral decision." Watson reddened, then laughed and said, "Well, if there are going to be any visceral decisions around here, I'd like to use my own viscera."

Recent research suggests that when making decisions, those at the top call more heavily on right-brain thinking than do managers at lower levels. Sound intuition helps form the successful CEO's perception. The inner ear hears what others may not. An inside voice may speak. Decisions are often said to come "from the heart."

Naturally, emotions must not be allowed to block or distort essential information. The CEO's capacity to achieve a balance between drawing upon emotions and reining them in may have much to do with developing CEO-class perceptiveness. Also, active, objective listening is crucial. One CEO I interviewed spoke of having become "an earnest listener." So, successful chiefs buttress their ability to observe and to listen earnestly with what they deeply feel in the gut. It is this highly developed degree of authentic perception that gives successful chief executives a firm grasp of actuality, a bedrock on which future plans will rest.

Team-building Skills

The successful CEO cannot afford to be alone at the top. One CEO told me that his company "extols the individual, but we celebrate the team."

Every person I interviewed mentioned the importance of the team, especially the top team. Because of its preeminent importance to the accomplishment of corporate objectives, its member executives deserve special attention from the chief in selection, assessment, coaching and, at times, removal.

Successful CEOs should have the ability to recognize their own strengths and shortcomings and to gather close to them individuals with complementary skills. These CEOs also recognize that when circumstances change drastically the make-up of the team must be reassessed.

Some chief executives operate best in tandem with a strong number-two person. Often this is the chief operating officer. Others find it more comfortable to disperse authority and accountability among several direct-reporting executives. Still others work through the shared responsibility of an office of the chairman, office of the president, or a corporate management committee. The particular configuration depends on several factors, including the personality and work habits of the chief, the particular talents of the most senior team members, and the career stage of the CEO. For example, if the chief is nearing retirement—and actively planning toward it—significant authority may be delegated to an heir apparent. In some cases, the soon-to-retire chief, with board concurrence , will begin delegating authority to as many as four potential successors. Sometimes this approach works but more often it invites the eventual losers to leave the company once the writing on the wall becomes painfully clear.

The job of chief executive has much to do with relationships, especially those with and among the members of the top team. While these relationships need initially to be defined with some clarity, they will be modified or modify themselves over time.

The skills and attitudes required for effective team building include:

■ An uncommon ability to judge talent.
■ A positive regard for team members.

- A capacity to communicate the company's context—both internally and externally.
- Willingness to encourage open and honest communication.
- Willingness to remove team members who are judged to be deficient—and to do it cleanly and humanely.

The chief is both leader and a member of the team and must be adept at playing both roles. This requires a capacity for accurate self-assessment and a commitment to the development of all team members, including oneself.

A strong team shares a high level of trust and candor and a low degree of insecurity or defensiveness. At best, its members communicate even without words; they share common goals and objectives, a common language, a bond, battle scars, mutual respect for each other, camaraderie, and commitment. Despite inevitable conflicts and rivalries, their doors and minds are open to one another.

Even with the best talent available, such a team does not just develop on its own. It is crafted and honed by the agenda-setting and interpersonal skills of the person at the top, skills the superior chief executive has in abundance.

Decisiveness Informed by Balanced Judgment

A tough-minded willingness to make hard decisions is a pervading quality shared by effective CEOs. But decisiveness alone isn't necessarily a virtue; it must be informed by balanced judgment. Successful CEOs are unwilling to spend days mulling over the pros and cons of an issue, so they make less important decisions quickly and quickly forget them. But they also avoid making important decisions prematurely. The men and women I interviewed seem quite comfortable, indeed happy, to be in the position of major decision-making, demonstrating supreme self-confidence in their judgment as they make dozens of decisions each day.

What is judgment? Peter Drucker notes that in a narrow sense every decision is a judgment. Each decision is "a choice between alternatives. It is rarely a choice between right and wrong. It is at best a choice between 'almost right' and 'probably wrong'—but much more often a choice between two courses of action, neither of which is probably more nearly right than the other."

In some jobs, the consequences of a decision can be known almost immediately. For example, the correctness of decisions made by air traffic controllers can be very quickly ascertained. When the controller leaves work each day, the results of all decisions made during that day are known. Those that must be made in the CEO's office are quite different. First, the information on which they must be based is imperfect. The chief executive often operates in an environment of ambiguity and uncertainty. Second, the decisions that must be made at the top are the tough ones. Finally, the "correctness" of long-range decisions—those that are properly delegated upward—may not be known for years. For example, the effectiveness of deciding to invest in the early phases of research and development cannot be measured until well after those efforts have borne fruit. The "rightness" of still other decisions can never be assessed with any certainty.

During the 1970s, as some conglomerate companies expanded rapidly by aggressively acquiring other companies, the judgment of their CEOs was rated positively by the business press. But in the 1980s, as some of those firms ran into financial difficulty or found their acquisitions to be ill-fitting, the quality of their earlier judgment was reassessed. These same firms proclaimed "the need to concentrate on our core business," as they sold off parts of their operation that had proved less than successful. Again, judgment at work, but in a new economic climate and certainly with more first-hand knowledge available. In both cases, backed by their boards of directors, the CEO exercised decisiveness. A chief may fail in many ways, but one way to fail with certainty is through indecisiveness.

It is instructive to consider the decision-making process of some occupants of that most demanding of all chief executive positions, the presidency of the United States. Dwight D. Eisenhower once described leadership as "the ability to decide what is to be done, and then to get others to want to do it." Richard M. Nixon wrote, "What lifts great leaders above the second-raters is that they are more forceful, more resourceful, and have a shrewdness of judgment that spares them the fatal error and enables them to identify the fleeting opportunity." Most would credit Richard Nixon with shrewdness and decisiveness. Yet during the Watergate period his judgment lacked the balance necessary to spare him "the fatal error."

Harry S Truman, thrust by the death of Franklin D. Roosevelt into office he did not seek, possessed the quality of decisiveness. During his presidency, Truman made many momentous decisions, including the decision to drop the atomic bomb. When he heard that General Marshall had gone to sleep at his usual time the night before D-Day, Truman said, "If you've done the best your can—if you have done what you have to do—there is no use worrying about it. . . . You can't think about how it would be . . . if you had done another thing. You have to decide."

Like U.S. Presidents, corporate CEOs "have to decide." The essential ingredient of balance in decision making comes partly from a deliberate exposure to varied points of view. Truman wrote, "I made it my business as President to listen to people in all walks of life and in all fields of endeavor and experience. I did not see only the people who ought to be seen—that is, those who were 'well-connected.' I always tried to be a good listener. But since the responsibility for making decisions had to be mine, I always reserved judgment."

Successful chief executives seek balanced advice but still need a perceptual objectivity to make a balanced decision. Possessing the will to decide, willing to live with their decisions, regardless of the result. While they insist on tough-mindedness in their people, they also hold themselves fully accountable for the consequences of their own decisions, right or wrong. In short, they exercise decisiveness informed by balanced judgment.

Strategic Focus

The CEOs I interviewed are pulling their companies into the future. Aware of changes in customer demand, alert to new technological developments, they constantly look for ways to reach out in new directions. Mediocre chief executives preside at their office in a reactive rather than proactive mode. Tending to the day-to-day problems of the firm, they may encourage their organization to find ways to do things better in the context of its current mission and market. The truly successful chief executive, however, operates in the transforming mode, creating a vision to guide the company into the future.

Although each transforming CEO creates a vision in his or her own way, certain common steps are followed. First is the diagnostic phase, which consists of a study into how the company got to where it is, then an inventory of the company's resources and capabilities, then a careful identification of gaps, which might be managerial or technological.

During the next phase, market niches are sought, new marketing approaches designed. A top management team is built, followed by intense discussions to gain team members' commitment to the need to redefine or reposition the company. The chief has the vital job of providing his or her company with intellectual capital.

Gradually the vision for the future becomes a plan. There is the inevitable need for additional resources, always in short supply. The successful chief will somehow find a way to obtain these resources. Some CEO's demand cost efficiencies within their own organizations to free up dollars for investment in new initiatives. Others use the strategy described by Peter Drucker as "creative abandonment," under which older, less successful parts of the business are sold off or closed down to provide funds needed for the future. Technological gaps may be overcome by hiring and internal search and development or through licensing or other external arrangement, such as joint venturing. If the gap is managerial, the CEO will not rest until he or she has identified or brought in the needed talent.

If the company's focus is to be changed dramatically, this must be articulated and the new vision sold to managers and employees at all levels. To get the word across, meetings must be held, speeches given, and the company's communications sharply coordinated. This new message is repeatedly trumpeted, the troops are rallied, and eventually the strategic vision for the future is accepted throughout the company by all who must implement it.

When this process is successful, the company becomes rejuvenated and reshaped. It clearly bears the stamp of the chief executive who provided the vision and the energies—the strategic focus—that made it all possible.

Tenacity

So far we have established that the successful CEO achieves a clear perception of reality, builds a strong team, exercises balance in decision making and creates a strategic focus. But one additional quality is essential: the determination to prevail through thick and thin.

Tenacity is an important component of any entrepreneurial venture; the job of a turnaround CEO demands it. It is equally required by the CEO who is attempting to point the corporation in new directions. Such a shift may call for major change in the corporate culture and the installation of new values. Bringing this about requires long and consistent effort by the CEO. The job of chief executive is physically and emotionally demanding, often exhausting. It requires the ability to absorb major disappointments, the resilience to bounce back, the determination to keep moving ahead. Most of those who make it to the top have had plenty of experience in dealing with adversity. In short, they are survivors. As corporate chiefs, they will experience still more adversity.

Once they reach the top, they require an even greater degree of tenacity. It is up to the chief executive to convey a positive outlook and to articulate a specific direction toward a favorable future even when business conditions are at their worst. Though most chiefs try to manage in a way that avoids surprises—especially negative ones—they arrive all too frequently. The successful chief learns to absorb these shocks and to help others to put the bad news behind them and move forward again.

Successful CEOs enjoy their jobs—not necessarily the power, but the challenge. The victories—large and small—seem to compensate for the occasional defeats.

The Indispensable Ingredient: Integrity

Underlying the skills and capabilities of successful chief executives is the essential quality of integrity. Without integrity, there can be no trust. Leadership is based on trust, and effective management fueled by it.

Integrity implies a wholeness, a completeness, an integration of values. Yet one person's values are not those of another. Through reflection a manager can develop an understanding of his or her own values; by actions and words, they can be understood by others. This is crucially important, for just as mangers dislike surprises, so do the people who work for and with them.

Personal integrity also implies a firm adherence to a system of ethics, a set of guiding beliefs that are gradually forged by each individual and repeatedly tested in the crucible of one's life. The wholeness of integrity demands, moreover, an integrated consistency of values, not the use of one set in the workplace and another at home. This implies an inner moral compass, a constancy, a conscience. (A child once defined conscience as the thing that feels bad when everything else feels good.) This inner alarm is critical to long-term success as a chief executive.

Integrity does *not* reside in the mouthing of pompous platitudes. Nor does it imply rigidity. Indeed, successful chief executives exercise great flexibility in their thoughts and actions, yet draw a clear line at ethical limits beyond which they will not go.

High offices have certainly been occupied by dishonest individuals. Some have taken unfair advantage of their power and position. Some still do; some always will. In 1985, for the first time, corporate officers were convicted of murder, in a bizarre case of an employee death caused by exposure to cyanide. And there are, moreover, some CEOs who—though their companies are not guilty of criminal behavior—achieve short-term success by less than ethical means. Despite these examples—which are, fortunately, exceptions—to be a successful chief executive over the *long* term requires the quality of integrity.

Reputations of companies are built on product quality, honest advertising, fairness in dealing with customers, sound community relationships, thoroughness in fulfilling governmental and other contracts, and truthful communications to employees and shareholders—in short, upon the fairness shown to all constituencies. It is only through the actual practice of integrity that the valuable asset of trust can be forged and maintained. Over the short-term, corners can be cut; over the long term of a manager's career, unprincipled actions will become very apparent.

The moral tone of any organization is set by its chief. If, in the executive office, a corner is cut here, a decision shaded there—no matter how high-flown the company's written code of ethics may be— uestionable conduct will soon develop at all levels. A chief executive cannot afford to wink at any breach of ethics, no matter how small. Like Caesar's wife, the chief must be beyond suspicion. Taken alone, integrity is no guarantee of a ticket to the top; but without it, that ticket is worthless.

When underpinned by integrity, the qualities I've described help to define the characteristics of successful CEOs. But these qualities by no means guarantee successful results—and boards of directors and shareholders will not forgive poor results over a long period. There are factors over which even the best CEOs may have no control. General economic forces represent one example. Another is a mismatch between the CEO and the industry (while some senior executives have succeeded in a variety of industries, they are few in number). But barring insurmountable factors, CEOs with the qualities described here lead their organizations and people to great accomplishments.

PART 4
THE WORLD
AROUND US:
PAST, PRESENT, AND
FUTURE

Leadership is studied in a number of environments and from divergent points of view. The military probably has been the subject of the most intense effort over a long period. Writers in business and government have been prolific in their attempts to characterize leadership. Academics from a variety of disciplines have proposed theory and conducted research in an attempt to "explain" leadership as well as to predict leadership success.

The missing element is an eclectic, multidisciplinary approach, representing the nature of our diverse society. Leaders do not come from a particular frame of reference. They reflect our cultural heritage and the many dimensions of life in and out of organizations.

For some reason, the study of history and literature has been lost as a way of learning about leadership. While we need not restrict ourselves to the study of leaders, it is important to examine the classical philosophical underpinnings of society if we want to grasp the assumptions relevant to human interrelationships and organizational evolution as we move into a new century. Western thought is a common base, although there has been a shift in immigration patterns in recent years that might make that less valid in the future. For now, Western culture prevails and gives us a solid grounding for appreciating our acceptance of leadership in the near term.

Perhaps we should not study leadership as a separate topic. In the pursuit of self-knowledge, a broader view may be more appropriate. Understanding why we act as we do may be better studied from a classical approach. Often, history points out that our present situation is a clone of past events. While that probably will help us predict the future, it will certainly help us understand the dynamics of successful leadership.

A View of the World

Regardless of the person, leaders seem to have a broader view of the world. It is helpful to thoroughly understand the microcosm of the organization, but the broad perspective helps put everything in context. To create a vision of the future, the leader must understand the total environment in which the organization exists. The more variety to choose from, the greater the number of options and combinations that are considered.

Arts and humanities allow the leader to develop the aesthetic component of values and feelings. It is not surprising that we often see successful leadership as a *passion*, a wellspring of emotion that keeps the leader directed toward the vision. If one sees the leader as producer-director, the metaphor comes alive. We serve a variety of people in organizations, and we need to relate to them culturally as well as professionally.

Leaders must synthesize many inputs in such a way that the *highest* common denominator is found. Finding what we value is the task of leadership. In the successful organization, the leader helps us achieve our personal goals while we strive to fulfill the goals of the group. How the leader relates to all of us depends on his or her breadth of knowledge.

Studying the classics provides the foundation on which today's actions are based. It is one thing to know *what* to do; it is another thing to understand *why* we do it. If leadership is based on the confidence of self-knowledge and introspection, then a thorough grounding in history, literature, the arts, and language is the best preparation.

Preparing for Leadership

One does not simply become a leader. There must be a real sense of preparation—by the individual as well as the institution. Clearly there is a setting for leadership that we refer to as the opportunity to lead. Organizations face opportunities and threats. These are the situations that determine the organization's future direction and are the elements of organizational survival, growth, and change. The challenge is to understand the setting for leadership. Careful study of the social landscape and architecture of the organizational setting tells a great deal about the leadership potential.

Often, people are simply "ready" for leadership. When an organization is drifting or faces a crisis in which no one seems able to cope, people start looking around for someone to lead them. Their search may be within or they may feel that the leader must come from outside the organization. There may be great dissatisfaction with the current leadership. Perhaps there are competing leaders, and the organization members are confused. The result is a subtle search for resolution, an implicit need for leadership.

But what of the potential leader? When the setting is right, the individual must be prepared to lead. Never underestimate the timing of situations. All too often, the opportunity for leadership emerges and the individual is not prepared or (worse) does not recognize the opportunity and fails to respond.

If there are no certain approaches to education and training in leadership, how does one prepare? Once again, we return to the idea of self-development. Our desire for leadership should be accompanied by an equivalent yearning to gain experience and study materials that help us understand our personal leadership qualities. There is a rich variety of choices. This seems to be a case where quantity and diversity of experience is the best preparation—so long as the focus is self-knowledge and development.

Leadership development is not a passive experience. One must actively engage the organization. Within the context of organizational structure, those people interested in developing their skills must ask questions and seek out opportunities and be aware of the historical context. There is some sense that personal development is self-initiated and self-directed. One must seek out jobs, education and training experience, mentors, advisors, and friends who will critique and give us feedback.

Leadership Education

In preparing for leadership, our view is that we need to teach people the joy of creating rather than all the sophisticated techniques of analyzing. Statistical models of the past are helpful in understanding what has happened (and, likely, why). But leadership is focused on the future. Creating the vision is the leader's challenge.

Wholistic approaches to organizational stability and change suggest the leader should be a generalist. The "world view" provides more possibilities to pursue. As decisions are developed, the wholistic leader understands all the second- and third-level implications. A decision to change the structure of an organization can impact the way customers and clients are treated. Reducing the training budget will eliminate costs but also will affect service levels and personnel development. Taking on an unrelated "business" may improve the financial outlook but may confuse people in terms of the company's overall mission, goals, and objectives. Leaders understand the inherent complexity of simplicity.

An appreciation of humanistic thought is the basis for understanding other points of view. In any organization, the more you understand the customers or clients, the better you can meet their needs. Sensitivity and caring are basic human values that serve our customers and clients, the public, and our employees. Integral to preparing people for leadership is the development of humanism.

Leadership Perspectives

In this section, we take a rather unusual approach. Four perspectives have been chosen. They were selected to develop the themes of classical preparation, historical appreciation, and the need for a broadly-based education. There are a number of practical examples and applications that support a humanistic approach to understanding the world around us.

"Lessons from Literature" by Ken Kovacs is a charge to study the permanence of leadership themes in the classics. Kovacs does not discount the popular writers, but he does give us several examples of how literature has more eloquently developed leadership over the years. He reminds us of how hard it is to forget Willy Loman.

In their book, *The Classic Touch*, John Clemens and Douglas Mayer provide a number of exciting linkages between the classics and modern leadership. We have selected "Plato: The Philosopher-Manager" as an especially articulate treatment of what we can learn from the classics. Perhaps the most important lesson here is the reminder that successful leaders do not have all the answers. Rather, they have mastered the discipline of asking the right questions.

"Bach to Basics" by Charles Smith is a delightful piece on harmony. From the genius of Bach's music we can learn a great deal about how various elements of an organization can be brought together with a central, pervasive theme (the vision, perhaps). Think of the metaphor of the leader as a composer, creating exciting new harmonies through the structure of the organization.

Because much corporate leadership training originates from business education, the last article, by Thomas Mulligan, ties it all together. "The Two Cultures in Business Education" suggests a restructuring of business education. Mulligan believes that the cultural elements of the humanities needs to be merged with contemporary education for the corporate world. We see this as the development of the intuitive *with* the rational, an interdependence of values. Interestingly, a 1988 study of business education repeats the challenge of this essay.

Leaders need to understand their organization and its tasks. At the same time, they must project a world view that acknowledges differences while creating a common vision. This is the challenge—depth and breadth. Nonetheless, it is all there for us to know. Are we willing to take the time to step away and reflect on our humanistic world? We must if we are to be the successful leaders of tomorrow.

13
LESSONS FROM LITERATURE

Ken Kovacs

Business and government decision-makers may turn to the words of Peter Drucker or Lee Iacocca when they need a little guidance. Management guru Tom Peter's fiery speeches also may command the attention of today's busy manager or administrator. But Plato or Shakespeare? What could they possibly have to offer?

Yet, a growing number of business educators and professional people are finding that great works of literature can indeed be a valuable learning tool. For example, in their recent book, *The Classic Touch: Lessons in Leadership from Homer to Hemingway*, two management professors from Hartwick College suggest that leading is much more than formulas and techniques, accounting and computers.

"Leaders work in a world where contradiction is commonplace, where today's right answer is tomorrow's disaster—a world in which hunch, intuition, experience and openness to untested ideas and certainly self-assurance are more important to success than mere technical skills," write John Clemens and Douglas Mayer. "The art of leading is the art of being human."

It's not surprising, they say, that books like Plutarch's *Lives*, Shakespeare's *King Lear* and Hemingway's *For Whom the Bell Tolls* offer rich perspectives on the job of leading.

"After all, the problems that are central to effective leadership—motivation, inspiration, sensitivity and communication—have changed little in the past 3,000 years. These problems were faced by the Egyptians when they built the pyramids, by Alexander when he created his empire, and by the Greeks when they battled the Trojans."

What separates great business leaders from the not-so-great, the authors say, often has more to do with "the classic touch"—the artistry of

Reprinted by permission from the *Golden Gate University Magazine*, 15:4 (October 1987), pp. 2-4.

getting others to commit themselves to their highest possible levels of achievement—than with specialized techniques.

"Knowledge of finance, marketing, production and personnel is important, of course; but it often produces the kind of leaders who, although able to name every single tree, may fail to notice that the forest is burning," Clemens and Mayer write. "What is needed is a broader view of leadership grounded in literature that focuses not on specialized techniques but rather on the vast human side of the leadership equation."

Harry Wolf, assistant professor in the Public Administration Program at Golden Gate University, put it another way.

> To me, the base point is that 80 to 90 percent of organizations are people: . . . . The material stuff is really a small part of it. If we don't learn how to deal with people, how can we ever hope to manage anything?

Wolf teaches a course titled "Public Administration in Literature," which offers an analysis and examination of administrative ideas and concepts through the use of fiction, plays, film, video, and poetry. Works by authors such as Sophocles, Shakespeare, More, Ibsen, Gogel, and Kafka are utilized, as well as those by contemporary authors. Administrative behavior, organizational dilemmas, management decision-making processes and interpersonal relationships are among the topics discussed.

Wolf often refers to a 1968 paper by Dwight Waldo, professor emeritus at Syracuse University, that offers a list of benefits that can be gained from literature. Published by the Institute of Governmental Studies at UC Berkeley, the paper, "The Novelist on Organization and Administration," suggests that literature helps to restore what professional-scientific literature necessarily omits or slights: the concrete, the sensual, the emotional, the subjective and the valuational.

Waldo lists the following specific benefits:

- Extending the range of our knowledge. "Vicarious experience can substitute for personal experience. One person's life is necessarily limited, but through the knowledge and skill of the artist he participates in many lives; in terms of our interest, we can learn about administration in times, countries and activities quite remote from personal experience."
- Through the eyes of the man of letters we can get a view of the administrator, more generally the Organization Man, as others view him. "Immersed in his world, continually viewing it from the inside, the Organization Man is apt to forget—if he ever knew—how he and

his organizational world appear to the outsider. And the views of the outsiders (and these outsiders may be in the organization but not of it) may be highly important data. In fact, that they certainly are important the professional literature increasingly recognizes. The view of the organization held by the man of letters will often strike the administrator as ignorant, shallow, precious or even hostile. But this only demonstrates the argument."

■ A desirable emotional stimulation or release. "I am not going to state it is a fact of psychology that treatments of administration which amuse or alternatively make angry or sad Administrative Man are 'good' for him. But I am in respectable company at least in arguing that through such mechanisms as identification and displacement, the practitioner or student can get relief from tension, achieve better emotional balance."

■ A better professional balance and humility. "Again, literature is not to be confused with Life, and its world is not the World. But certainly this view of the World is larger, more varied, more rounded, than that of any single student or practitioner. If we are ready to receive the 'message' we can gain a useful sense of the limits of what we know and are able to control."

■ Through literary treatments we can come more closely to grips with the psychological and moral aspects of administrative decision-making. "In literary creations or recreations of administrative situations the subjective 'feel' of a difficult decision that, inevitably, determines the lives and fortunes of flesh-and-blood people is sometimes superbly well conveyed."

■ Through good literary treatments of administration one can achieve wisdom. "At their best literary treatments convey a rounded and balanced picture of an activity at the center of the contemporary world, of the conflict and blending of good and evil, of the commingling of the rational and the irrational, of the absurd jostling of the significant and noble by the trivial and petty, of high achievement shadowed and suffused by an unescapabe element of tragedy."

One of the most popular works used to illustrate how today's leaders in business and government can learn from literature is Shakespeare's *King Lear*. Clemens and Mayer suggest that the story "strikingly illustrates the folly of ill-conceived succession, sloppy decentralization, and thoughtless delegation." Wolf is more blatant.

"It's an example of a bad manager," he said. "Here's a manager that had decided to turn over management to his subordinates, his daughters. He hasn't thought it through, he thinks he knows his daughters.

He divides his kingdom between two daughters and they immediately turn around and rob him of his kingdom. It's a lousy management decision."

An extension of this literary approach to teaching management and leadership is the group workshop in which professionals discuss certain literary works with their peers. Seven years ago Brandeis University, at the request of the chief justice of the Massachusetts District Court System, developed a program for judges in which literature was used to explore various ethical dilemmas, role tensions and career crises commonly associated with "burnout."

"Although the program was originally thought to be addressed to law issues (and dealt with issues of judgment, justice, the tension between private conscience and public obligation, etc.), it soon became apparent that the heart of the program was the way in which it allowed professionals to explore with one another, in a candid and supportive setting, how it felt to exercise power and responsibility in our society," said Sanford Lotter, director of continuing studies at Brandeis. Lotter established the program with Saul Touster, director of legal studies.

"It was an easy step to go from judges to physicians and then from physicians to public service professionals and on to organization executives and so forth," Lotter said.

After six years in existence, the Brandeis program, now known as "Humanities and the Professions," has a faculty of 35 from more than 10 different Massachusetts institutions of higher education and sixteen in six other states, according to Lotter. Generally, the program is designed to address contemporary social issues, broad historical and cultural contexts and the difficult value dilemmas professionals encounter daily in their practice.

"The many very favorable responses we have received from participants attest to the need for and value of such a program for those who carry out important roles in our society," Lotter said.

Wolf participated as a leader in such a workshop conducted in June at Stanford University. He was among 14 professors who served as discussion leaders in the day-long seminars. Two professors worked with groups of 16 or 17 participants, all from the Northern California Grantmakers. Three works of literature were discussed, including *King Lear*, *The Guest* by Albert Camus, and Leo Tolstoy's *The Death of Ivan Ilych*.

"The main reaction by participants was that they said they felt stimulated and very excited," Wolf said. "It was like getting mental exercise. Secondly, I think they got a sense of being able to look at something and read it and relate it to their situation. Many of them said how relevant the material was to some of their management problems."

Caitland Croughan, associate director of the California Council for the Humanities, which coordinated the workshop with Brandeis and Stanford, said discussing literary works with others in your profession takes the learning a step further.

"I have bought into the old Socratic method," she said. "That is, you don't make intellectual progress except by sharing your sincere beliefs in public. Even the process of having to communicate to someone else your deeply held beliefs is beneficial. I am convinced that there is no comparison with talking about a book with someone else who has read it."

Croughan said many people perceive the whole thing as frivolous until they actually experience it.

"Even then, people find it hard to explain it," she said. "But I think the program taps into a hunger these professionals have to discuss their problems. The way we have constructed our life in Western society we don't have time to reflect on conflict. Through these workshops people can use great literary works to look into themselves."

There are some business executives and administrators who are convinced they have little to gain from reading and discussing literature. Anthony Branch, vice president for academic affairs at GGU, said one possible reason for this resistance is that historically the world of business has been separate from the world of intellectuals and artists.

"And in modern fiction businessmen, generally, have not been portrayed sympathetically," he added.

Clemens and Mayer explain how the two worlds, both in literature and reality, are intertwined.

"Homer's Achilles, Shakespeare's Othello, Miller's Willy Loman— these people have 'been there,' struggling with the same kinds of sticky, intractable, often maddening leadership problems that you face every day. You can learn from their victories—and their defeats— because the lessons learned by the authors who created these characters permeate much of what they've written. Plato's *Republic* contains more insights and lessons for leaders than any textbook. Besides being one of history's great philosophers, Plato was a down-to-earth, hands-on leader with a proven track record of successful innovation. . . . Clearly, there is nothing ancient about Plato's thinking; he is a kindred spirit, if not a true contemporary, of today's best leaders."

14
PLATO: THE
PHILOSOPHER-MANAGER

John K. Clemens and Douglas F. Mayer

When Alfred North Whitehead said that the West's philosophical tradition consists merely of a series of footnotes to "him," he was referring to Plato, the Greek philosopher born in 428 B.C. Another devotee, Ralph Waldo Emerson, had rhapsodized a century before Whitehead: "Burn all the libraries, for their value is in this one book." Emerson was referring to Plato's most famous work, *The Republic.*

These laudatory opinions of Plato are almost universally shared. He along with Socrates, his teacher, and Aristotle, his student, laid the philosophical foundations of Western culture. Plato developed a discerning and wide-ranging system of thought that was at once ethical, mystical, and rational. Against the profound intellectual confusion and moral chaos following Athens' defeat in the Peloponnesian War, Plato's philosophical system offered the solace of absolute ethical principles: a strong anchor, as it were, against turbulent and frightening change. Indeed, if the Periclean Age had been all that its supporters claimed it was, or if the Peloponnesian War had not sapped Athenian will, Plato's greatest dialogues might never have been written.

But Plato did write—prodigiously. His dialogues, after 2,400 years, are still incomparable studies of the basic issues that confront human beings. They offer even more—particularly to those who manage and lead—because their author was not only a consummate philosopher but also an accomplished manager, innovator, and entrepreneur. The school he established in Athens in 387 B.C. as an institute for the systematic pursuit of philosophical and scientific research was an entrepreneurial triumph, lasting more than 500 years. It was a true educational innovation in that tedious lecturing was mercifully not allowed.

Reprinted by permission from *The Classic Touch: Lessons in Leadership from Homer to Hemingway,* John K. Clemens and Douglas F. Mayer, Dow Jones Irwin (1987), pp. 37–49.

Instead, students, egged on by their teachers, discussed, argued, and analyzed "problems," much as their 20th-century counterparts come to grips with cases at many business schools today.

The only biographical knowledge we have of Plato comes from some of his letters. We know that he had a refined palate and enjoyed the art of living life to its fullest, as became an aristocratic Greek, and that he was a man of exquisite taste with a great love of beauty. Plato was blessed with a keen mind and a good sense of humor. In short, Plato possessed all of the accoutrements that one might expect in a successful young man. He wasted none of them. At 25, he was a poet and playwright. At 40, he had founded his Academy. By the end of his life (he died in his 80s), he had written more than 35 works. As a young man, Plato had his heart set on a career in politics. But he soon became disenchanted with this idea. Why he turned to philosophy is evident in one of his letters:

> I, who had at first been full of eagerness for a public career, as I gazed upon the whirlpool of public life and saw the incessant movement of shifting currents, at last felt dizzy . . . and finally saw clearly in regard to all states now existing that without exception their system of government is bad.

This critical appraisal of the human condition animated much of Plato's philosophy. Especially in his later life, Plato was motivated largely by frustration and even despair. The disastrous Peloponnesian War affected him deeply, as had the death of his mentor, Socrates. He was infuriated by the incompetence of Pericles' successors, and he was outraged by the rising influence of Sparta, whose culture was almost the opposite of that of Athens.

History's First Consultant's Report

Plato was a reformer. He sought to change Athens, just as any contemporary manager wants to "turn around" a troubled organization. This is what makes Plato's most famous dialogue, *The Republic*, superb reading for managers as well as philosophers. It is history's first consultant's report to the leaders of an organization that is being badly beaten by the competition.

The Republic was a response to this catastrophic management failure. In it, Plato argued against the management style of Periclean Athens. He saw it as a kind of destructive imbalance, a style of managing in which self-serving individual interests could too easily overwhelm the needs of the organization. He challenged assumptions about management and leadership that were as voguish in ancient Athens as they are in our society, reaffirmed others, and established wholly new ones. *The*

Republic focuses on Plato's critical appraisal of democratic management and provides an excellent example of Socratic dialectic.

"Democratic" Management: Plato's Second Opinion

Managing "democratically" has been at the heart of American management since the 1960s. Although individual interpretations vary somewhat, there is a common thread: managers are exhorted to become more people-oriented, and employees are encouraged to participate in decision making. The goal is the de-emphasis of "top-down," autocratic decision making in favor of a "bottom-up," participative style.

Democratic management has been an appealing, and uniquely American, idea. In line with the West's egalitarian political philosophy, it has been programmed into corporate cultures by management consultants, professed by business school teachers, and touted in corporate training programs. Its most influential devotee, 20th-century behavioral scientist Douglas McGregor, has been permanently enshrined in the pantheon of management scholars.

But Does Democratic Management Work?

Plato's reservations about the effectiveness of democratic leadership in fifth-century B.C. Athens may be useful to consider today. Whether or not one agrees with Plato's criticism of democratic management, his position provides a provocative "second opinion." Plato had been deeply offended by the immoderation of radical Athenian democracy. He had observed Athenian leaders being seduced into giving the people whatever they wanted. Athens was moving increasingly in the direction of becoming a welfare state. Plato saw thousands of jurors, councilors, and major and minor officials and others gaining their livelihood from the public coffers. The boom in government buildings provided not only jobs, but also a rich architectural legacy that far outlasted the state institutions that the buildings were designed to house. In sum, the state's services became an entitlement, having been transformed from an activity that most could not afford to one that they welcomed and later demanded.

Plato's often critical perspective on democratic management can be better understood against this troublesome background. He believed that although radical democracy may have been effective during Athens' Golden Age, it was an unalloyed disaster once storm clouds appeared on the horizon. He saw that a new kind of leader—a "philosopher-king"—might be the only solution.

Plato's critique of democratic management was wide-ranging. He feared the leadership of amateurs over professionals, the rise of excessive individualism, and the diffusion of responsibility that is the inevitable result of management by committee. More than anything else, he was haunted by the fear that radical democracy would inevitably lead to the appointment of leaders who cared more about flattering the mob than about doing what was right.

Citizens, Plato noted, were often not the best judges of who should lead. Nowhere are these doubts better described than in his parable of the ship's navigator:

> The sailors are quarreling over the control of the helm. . . . They do not understand that the genuine navigator can only make himself fit to command a ship by studying the seasons of the year, sky, stars, and winds, and all that belongs to his craft; and they have no idea that, along with the science of navigation, it is possible for him to gain, by instruction or practice, the skill to keep control of the helm whether some of them like it or not. If a ship were managed in that way, would not those on board be likely to call the expert in navigation a mere star-gazer, who spent his time in idle talk and was useless to them?

Plato's ship is like any organization wracked by factionalism. People mill around waiting for someone to take charge, often choosing the most popular, but not the best qualified, among them as leader. Like the true navigator in the parable, the most competent candidate for manager will rarely be selected by the employees.

One Organization versus Many

Plato believed that radical democracy would inevitably lead to chaos, resulting in an organization made up of "many organizations," in which each would go its own independent way:

> Now what is the character of this new regime? Obviously the way they govern themselves will throw light on the democratic type of man.
>
> No doubt.
>
> First of all, they are free. Liberty and free speech are rife everywhere; anyone is allowed to do what he likes.
>
> Yes, so we are told.
>
> That being so, every man will arrange his own manner of life to suit his pleasure. The result will be a greater variety of individuals than under any other constitution. So it may be the finest of all, with its variegated pattern of all sorts of characters. Many people may think it the best, just as women and children might admire a mixture of colours of every shade in the pattern of a dress. . . . There is so much tolerance and superiority to petty considerations; such a contempt for all those fine principles we laid down in founding our commonwealth, as when we said that only a very exceptional nature

could turn out a good man, if he had not played as a child among things of beauty and given himself only to creditable pursuits. A democracy tramples all such notions under foot; with a magnificent indifference to the sort of life a man has led before he enters politics, it will promote to honour anyone who merely calls himself the people's friend.

Plato believed that in management—of states or other organizations—someone has to take responsibility. Someone has to call the shots and lead. This does not mean that managers or other leaders have to be callous, thoughtless, or inhumane. It does, however, require singleness of purpose, loyalty to a vision of what the organization is to become, and a great deal of self-discipline.

The Need for Benevolent Tyrants

Plato was perceptive enough to see that leading must sometimes be a solo act, that leaders must be more concerned with the good of the enterprise than with pleasing the multitude. On those frequent occasions when the two are compatible, an easygoing, democratic, management-by-consensus style works and works well. But Plato knew that when the going gets tough, it might be time for a benevolent tyrant to take the helm.

A tough-minded leader might have saved Studebaker, the now-defunct automobile company. There are striking parallels between the downfall of Studebaker and the ancient clash of democratic Athens and autocratic Sparta. Studebakers' demise was caused by its interest in furthering industrial democracy rather than in meeting the developing threat from General Motors. Managing by committee and making excessive concessions to its unions, Studebaker lost sight of its economic objectives. Meanwhile, GM focused with Spartan tenacity on the business survival. Its authoritarianism worked. Today, GM is the largest automaker in the world. Studebaker went out of business in 1964.

Consider a more recent example. Apple Computer practiced radical democratic and egalitarian management under Steven Jobs's leadership during Silicon Valley's heyday. But when IBM launched its personal computer, the "good ol' days" were gone forever. Jobs wisely brought in John Sculley, from Eastern-establishment PepsiCo, who immediately put an end to laissez-faire management at Apple. At a meeting of financial analysts just before Jobs departed, Sculley threw down the gauntlet: "There is," he said, "no role for Steven Jobs in the operations of Apple now or in the future." He did not ask for a show of hands. Described as a manager who can be tough, even ruthless, Sculley is clearly in charge at Apple. A recent statement that he made says it all: "I am alone at the top now."[1]

As Plato suggested, democratic management is not a cure-all. It is not the only style of management that works. Often there's no time for a vote. Even if there is, like the ships' crew in Plato's parable, employees may not know enough about what it is they are voting on to make the wisest choice. Good management is sometimes a solo act, relying less on democratic consensus than on individual judgment.

Nurturing Disagreement: Managing "Socratically"

Socrates, who lived from 470 B.C. to 399 B.C., was Plato's intellectual inspiration, teacher, and friend and the leading character in his dialogues. History views Socrates enthusiastically, and not unjustifiably, as the paragon of philosophy and its true father. But, as is often the case, his contemporaries were less impressed and quite unconscious of his greatness. To them he was, quite simply, the town character. Many wrote him off as an obtrusive bore due to his penchant for assaulting them with embarrassing questions. As if this were not enough Socrates claimed to be under the guidance of a special "voice," declaring that he had received messages from the Delphic Oracle—an assertion that greatly increased both his local importance and his notoriety. He was a popular pedagogue who gathered around him a clique of young disciples. Together they frequented Athens' marketplace and outtalked all but their sturdiest companions.

As self-appointed gadfly, Socrates spent most of his life causing no end of trouble in complacent Athens. By questioning, cajoling, wheedling, and prodding, he forced Athenians to think and to question beliefs that they had taken for granted. This finally got him into trouble. The Athenians charged him with impiety toward the gods and corrupting the youth. He was thrown into prison, tried, and sentenced to death. After a month, during which he refused friends' offers to help him escape, Socrates drank a cup of hemlock and died.

The Importance of Questioning

Socrates left mankind an immensely valuable legacy—the "Socratic method" of question and answer. He was firmly convinced that the human mind could arrive at virtue and truth only through a process of questioning and discussion. He was, above all else, an incomparable questioner and an exceptional listener—perhaps the best arguer the world has ever known. He knew that asking the right questions was far more important than getting the right answers. Questioning was Socrates' way of getting at the truth, at the core of a problem. Using dialectic, he would examine opinions or ideas logically and from many different points of view, much as a jeweler looks at a gem from many different angles in order to determine its value.

In *The Republic*, Plato's characters are invariably trying to discover the truth through the use of dialectic. One states an opinion. Another criticizes it. This dialogue takes a lot of time. The impatient reader gets the idea that Plato's characters, unlike busy managers, have all the time in the world. They go off on what seem to be irrelevant tangents. There is no agenda. No schedule. And there are many "meetings." In other words, dialectic not only requires Job-like patience but also seems to be the opposite of "good management."

An Example of Managing by Asking Questions

In *The Republic*, Socrates' dialogue with Polemarchus on the meaning of justice demonstrates dialectic in action. A member of the group, Simonides, has already argued that justice means "giving every man his due." Socrates argues that Simonides surely did not mean it "just," for example, to return dangerous weapons to a madman simply because they were owed to him. Notice how, through the process of cross-examination, Socrates gets Polemarchus to make certain admissions, then step by step draws him on, and finally leads him to draw an absurd conclusion—which exposes the fallacy of his argument.

> It is certainly hard to question the inspired wisdom of a poet like Simonides; but what this saying means you may know, Polemarchus, but I do not. Obviously it does not mean that we were speaking of just now—returning something we have been entrusted with to the owner even when he has gone out of his mind. And yet surely it is his due, if he asks for it back?
> Yes.
> But it is out of the question to give it back when he has gone mad?
> True.
> Simonides, then, must have meant something different from that when he said it was just to render a man his due.
> Certainly he did.

Socrates then shows that Simonides' definition of justice, to "return that which is owed," cannot apply in this case, since only "good" is due from one friend to another.

> And what about enemies? Are we to render whatever is their due to them?
> Yes, certainly, what really is due to them; which means, I suppose, what is appropriate to an enemy—some sort of injury.
> It seems, then that Simonides was using words with a hidden meaning, as poets will. He really meant to define justice as rendering to everyone what is appropriate to him; only he called that his "due."
> Well, why not?

Now Polemarchus changes the course of the discussion to the meaning of justice among enemies.

> His idea was that, as between friends, what one owes to another is to do him good, not harm.
>
> I see, said I; to repay money entrusted to one is not to render what is due, if the two parties are friends and the repayment proves harmful to the lender. That is what you say Simonides meant?
>
> Yes, certainly.

At this point, Socrates satirizes the common Greek belief that justice consists of helping one's friends and harming one's enemies, by constructing an analogy, between justice and the arts. He leads Polemarchus to conclude that the "work" of justice is the giving of good to friends and evil to enemies, just as the "work" of medicine gives health to human bodies:

> But look here, said I. Suppose we could question Simonides about the art of medicine—whether a physician can be described as rendering to some object what is due or appropriate to it; how do you think he would answer?
>
> That the physician administers the appropriate diet or remedies to the body.
>
> And the art of cookery—can that be described in the same way?
>
> Yes; the cook gives the appropriate seasoning to his dishes.
>
> Good. And the practice of justice?
>
> If we are to follow those analogies, Socrates, justice would be rendering services or injuries to friends or enemies.
>
> So Simonides means by justice doing good to friends and harm to enemies?
>
> I think so.
>
> And in matters of health who would be the most competent to treat friends and enemies in that way?
>
> A physician.
>
> And on a voyage, as regards the dangers of the sea?
>
> A ship's captain.
>
> In what sphere of action, then, will the just man be the most competent to do good or harm?
>
> In war, I should imagine; when he is fighting on the side of his friends and against his enemies.
>
> I see. But when we are well and staying on shore, the doctor and the ship's captain are of no use to us.
>
> True. It is also true that the just man is useless when we are not at war.
>
> I should not say that.

Polemarchus is subsequently reduced to asserting that the "work" of justice is the safekeeping of money when it is not being used. That is, justice does not serve a very important function:

> So justice has its uses in peace-time too?
> Yes.
> Like farming, which is useful for producing crops, or shoemaking, which is useful for providing us with shoes. Can you tell me for what purposes justice is useful or profitable in time of peace?
> For matters of business, Socrates.
> In a partnership, you mean?
> Yes.
> But if we are playing draughts, or laying bricks, or making music, will the just man be as good and helpful a partner as an expert draught-player, or a builder, or a musician?
> No.
> Then in what kind of partnership, will he be more helpful?
> Where money is involved, I suppose.
> Except, perhaps, Polemarchus, when we are putting our money to some use. If we are buying or selling a horse, a judge of horses would be a better partner; or if we are dealing in ships, a shipwright or a sea-captain.
> I suppose so.
> Well, when will the just man be specially useful in handling our money?
> When we want to deposit it for safe-keeping.
> When the money is to lie idle, in fact?
> Yes.
> So justice begins to be useful only when our money is out of use?
> Perhaps so.

Socrates, using dialectic, has led Polemarchus to recognize the vagueness of his—and Simonides'—ideas about justice by demonstrating to him the absurdity of his initial conclusions.

Socratic Management at Anheuser-Busch

Likewise managers can adapt Socratic dialectic to improve critical thinking and the quality of communications in their organizations. That is what has happened at Anheuser-Busch, where August Busch III, the chairman and CEO, has assumed the role of Socratic manager. Busch encourages openness in his nine-member executive committee. He runs it Socratically, insisting that each member present his opinion and then back it up. When really tough decisions are on the agenda, Busch stages formal debates—he calls them "dialectics"—at which two executives take opposing points of view. These executives are given small staffs and several weeks to prepare their cases. It seems to work; Anheuser-Busch is the world's leading brewery.[2]

Peter Drucker, in *The Effective Executive,* also endorses the use of Socratic dialetic in management. "Decisions of the kind the executive has to make," he says, "are not made well by acclamation. They are made well only if based on the clash of conflicting views, the dialogue between different points of view, the choice between different judgments. The first rule in decision making is that one does not make a decision unless there is disagreement."[3] Alfred P. Sloan, the man who revitalized General Motors in the 1920s when it was close to bankruptcy, appreciated the value of dialogue versus monologue. At a meeting of one of his top committees, everyone assented to the proposal being considered. "Gentlemen, " retorted Sloan, "I take it we are all in complete agreement on the decision here." Everyone around the conference table nodded. "Then," he continued, "I propose we postpone further discussion on this matter until our next meeting to give ourselves time to develop disagreement and perhaps gain some understanding of what the decision is all about."

Nurture Disagreement; Nurture Dialogue

The lesson of all this is to avoid the managerial monologue and to engage instead in dialogue. Leadership, it turns out, is surprisingly similar to philosophy. It requires engaged inquiry. Like the participants in Plato's dialogues, leaders must get people to feel the challenge of a problem that involves them. Only dialogue makes this possible. Policy manuals and detailed procedures cannot replace the spirited inquiry that is consistently produced via dialogue. It's important, too, to learn to listen and to question. This may sound simple, but it is very hard to do. Most managers lecture. They tell. This has its place, of course, for they must pass on their experience to others. As an information-disseminating device, the monologue works reasonably well. But as a problem-solving device, it is a disaster.

Socratic dialogue is a learnable communication strategy of immense importance to leaders. It is *the* critical element in a strong, centralized management system like the one Plato advocated. It enables the whole organization system, from "philosopher-manager" to newest employee, to get to the truth. The organization's history, experience, and "truths" are passed down from executives to junior managers through dialogue. And the junior manager's perceptions of his or her problems are similarly passed up the organization. Dialogue demands one-on-one communications. It demands feedback. It demands that cherished assumptions be continually challenged. And it "licenses" tough-minded management that is based on fact, not opinion.

Notes

1. *Business Week,* January 27, 1986, p. 96.
2. *Business Week,* February 17, 1986, p. 58.
3. Peter Drucker, *Effective Executive,* p. 148.

15
BACH TO
BASICS

Charles Smith

I*n the architecture of my music I want to demonstrate to the world the architecture of a new and beautiful social commonwealth. The secret of my harmony? I alone know it. Each instrument is counterpoint, and (there are) as many contrapuntal parts as there are instruments. It is the enlightened self-discipline of the various parts, each voluntarily imposing on itself the limits of its individual freedom for the well-being of the community. This is my message. Not the autocracy of a single stubborn melody on the one hand. Or the anarchy of unchecked noise on the other. No, a delicate balance between the two; an enlightened freedom.*

—Johann Sebastian Bach

Johann Sebastian Bach's accomplishments in the world of music were inspired by the same goal pursued by corporate America—to create order amid chaos without squelching the adaptability that maximizes creativity. We could better understand the dynamics of creativity in organizations, especially large and complex organizations, if we listened to Bach.

His music displays tremendous creativity, wisdom, sophistication, and a vision of possibility. And although Bach first composed within the traditional structures of his time, he was futuristic. He used structure, paradox, conflict, discord, and dissonance to build greater harmony, present new ways of viewing older themes, and create completely new themes not limited by the past. If that sounds familiar it's because forward-thinking organizations are trying to do just that.

Musical Architecture

Bach's work represents a unique blend of science and art. Each composition exhibits systematic development and, at the same time, crea-

Reprinted by permission from *New Management*, 5:2 (Fall 1987) pp. 4-7. Copyright 1987 by John Wiley & Sons, Inc. All rights reserved.

tivity and variety that defies categorization. (Unfortunately for his students, Bach's unique style did not allow them to learn a few pieces, master his style, and easily play the rest of his works. They had to learn his compositions the old-fashioned way: one at a time.)

In many ways, Bach had the ideal creative marketing orientation. He looked beyond superfluous wants—much of the music of Bach's time was shallow and uninspiring—and sought to fulfill the needs of the listener at a deeper level.

In fact, Bach was determined to create his own audience and subtly shape its taste. He believed that listeners wanted more than they realized.

Although he created melodies that continue to satisfy many tastes, Bach did not concern himself with pandering to individual tastes. Instead, he moved in a direction that modern executives often fear and avoid: he played to a future audience.

Creative Freedom

Bach knew the works of his contemporaries and predecessors inside and out and drew on them when necessary (to produce a traditional piece for his parish church, for example). But the traditional systems and mode of his day frustrated him because he knew he needed to increase his resources to express his creative impulses. Although he placed heavy emphasis on creative patterns, he invariably broke free of the structure. For instance, he adopted and refined the existing system of counterpoint to expand his range of possibilities.

Obviously, melodies are the basic structures of Bach's works. But he refused to be limited by the melody from only bass and strings which, he believed, produced mechanistic homophony. By playing different melodies simultaneously, then counterpointing them, and, finally, creating resolution, Bach moved from the predictable to a world of many possibilities.

Counterpoint

The creative organization must use structure and operating procedures much as Bach used melody—as forces that indicate direction but don't hamper innovation. So, too, must an organization recognize counterpoint, which, in the business world, translates into the acceptance of conflict as an opportunity. Corporate executives must allow different points of view and bring them together so their resolution can bring a new richness to an organization.

And these same executives must encourage flexibility. The activity that commands center-stage attention today may be less important at another time, particularly when an organization is faced with the requirements of today's global economy.

Dealing with differences, confrontation, and conflict is a tough assignment. As differences increase, harmony seems impossible to attain. Other than the shortsighted use of force, there seems only one solution to this dilemma. As in Bach's highly structured but progressive and fluid fugues, each single part of the organization must be simultaneously yielding and strong, able to bring about a free and flowing melody, and yet still retain its own individual and unique contribution.

The New Order

Corporate culture frequently inhibits harmony and stifles innovation. But Bach understood how to challenge culture. His musical innovations often break in unexpectedly and seem out of place. Indeed, his discontinuous leads from the established order may cause the listener some discomfort.

How did Bach resolve this tension? By linking the seemingly discontinuous innovation with the old order. He returned to original melodies and carried them forward, step by step, until they reached a point where they harmonized, or were somehow associated with the new.

This method of dealing with innovation is valuable for organizations, too. Research on successful innovators indicates that they are frequently perceived as erroneous, radical, unrealistic, and too far removed from an organizations' day-to-day realities, especially when they are introducing new ideas, proposals, and suggestions for future directions within their companies. The same research suggests that, if the perspectives of innovators are recognized and combined with old ingredients, their ideas ultimately become the sources of new directions and development for organizations.

Bach's Guidelines

Are there guidelines for a company that wants to recognize and respect the old order and validate the new? The following characteristics of Bach's music are a start:

1. He didn't allow a single melody to predominate.
2. He saw differences and discord as sources of greater order. Instead of trying to maintain a steady, ongoing theme, he utilized the skilled management of dialectic, difference, and even dissonance or chaos to attain greater harmony and creativity. He developed contrapuntal intensity, in which each part preserved its independence and individuality.

3. Bach used transgression of convention to produce a new order, but this transgression did not discard themes and relationships that had been previously established. His work frequently shattered musical conventions, yet his music is not totally discontinuous from that of his predecessors.

4. A respect for form permeates Bach's music. He emphasized creativity and departures from existing orders, but complex blueprints, centralizing structures, and mathematical proportion were essential to his works.

5. Bach took advantage of state-of-the-art technology and resources. He mastered the works of his predecessors and contemporaries and knew when to draw upon techniques and styles. He understood his own limits and knew when it was necessary to look to others for guidance.

6. The sources of Bach's innovation were intuition and experimentation. Bach often shocked the great masters (who tuned his instruments) with his unorthodox behavior. He plucked strings and danced on organ foot pedals in what seemed to be illogical and incomprehensible ways, and produced harmonies that the masters never dreamed were possible.

7. Bach's music was the result of ideals rather than the prevalent tastes of his audience and was grounded in a societal vision.

8. His methods of training emphasized freedom, self-discovery, and discipline, and were based on presenting students with concrete goals and honest feedback about progress. Bach allowed his pupils to make errors and discover their obstacles to progress. He demanded great discipline, and yet strove to be continually aware of their struggles, doing whatever he could to make the learning process less tedious. Almost all of his students became prominent musicians, composers or musical scholars; some were better received than Bach was in his time.

A New Perspective

If there is one central message that Bach left us, it is that harmony is a possibility even amid an infinite number of different notes and themes—that it is a realistic and attainable organizational goal.

To apply this message to their organizations, corporate executives must share a vision that stakeholders can identify with. That vision serves two key purposes:

■ It is a point of resolution among the varying interests, ideals, and characteristics of the stakeholders. Bach believed that if there was significant overlap between the complete vision (or the organization's vision) and the contribution of the individual (the organizational participant), individual self-interest would become "enlightened," and take on a new meaning, an expansion of self and identification with the whole instead of simply with parts of the whole.

■ It supplies a cohering force which the organization can use when it deals with change.

The development of a greater harmony requires some stretching and wrenching of the status quo. And this uprooting can be disastrous if a company lacks vision. But Bach's philosophy can serve to inspire vision, too. After all, his message was "not the autocracy of a single stubborn melody" nor "the anarchy of unchecked noise." He strove for "a delicate balance between the two; an enlightened freedom. The harmony of the stars in the heavens, the yearning for brotherhood in the heart of man. This is the secret of my music."

16
THE TWO CULTURES IN BUSINESS EDUCATION

Thomas M. Mulligan

Thirty-one years ago, the British physicist-turned-novelist C. P. Snow characterized the line of demarcation between the scientific culture and the culture of the humanities. "The separation between the two cultures," he wrote, "has been getting deeper under our eyes; there is precious little communication between them, little but different kinds of incomprehension and dislike" (1956, p. 413).

Snow's essay has generated much discussion concerning whether this deep division really exists. In this paper, it is argued that the division between the two cultures is indeed real in business education and that Snow may even have underestimated its seriousness and the difficulty of reconciliation. Nevertheless, both cultures should be represented in business education, and a principal mission for the discipline of business ethics should be to provide a humanities-based counterbalance to what is now an almost entirely science-based education.

Contemporary Business Education

"The first thing, impossible to miss," Snow continued, "is that scientists are on the up and up" (1956, p. 413). Certainly, in recent decades, business research and teaching have moved progressively in the direction of science. The landmark studies of business education by Pierson (1959) and by Gordon and Howell (1959) have had great influence. The often unsubstantiated descriptive content of earlier business school curricula and research has been replaced by quantitative description based on rigorous data collection, computer-assisted mathematical modeling, and the foundational concepts of science—testable hypotheses (or, or least, testable networks of hypotheses), correlated observations, and causal explanations.

Reprinted by permission from the *Academy of Management Review*, 12:4 (1987), pp. 593-599.

Pierson's view of the scientific character of proper business research was unequivocal:

> The broad purpose of business research may be said to be to increase the fund of scientific knowledge about the operations of the individual firm. To this end business schools need to concentrate on developing a body of widely applicable generalizations which have been scientifically tested and can be used in developing still further knowledge in this area. The significance of any given piece of research depends on how much it contributes to this objective (1959, p. 313).

Similarly, the whole objective of Gordon and Howell's recommendations was to improve the conformity of business school research to the requirements of rigorous science:

> Thus the business schools need to develop . . . more applied research at a higher analytical level . . . [which] implies the formulation of challenging hypotheses, the development and use of more sophisticated analytical tools, including more utilization of concepts and findings from the various social sciences and greater reliance on the tools of mathematics and statistics, and the systematic collection of detailed and reliable data (1959, p. 382).

In their teaching program for undergraduate business education, Gordon and Howell (1959) saw a place for "the more relevant branches of history and, perhaps, philosophy" (p. 65) as well as literature, language, fine arts, and foreign culture. However, they recommended that only 12 of the 120 undergraduate semester units be devoted to the humanities, adding "we cannot rationalize any specific requirement from this group" (p. 157). Because of the concern of educators and employers about student competence in communication, they recognized the usefulness of English composition, literature, and speech, and recommended that 12 to 15 undergraduate semester units be required in these areas (pp. 154-156). At the MBA level, however, they proposed no requirement or elective from any humanities discipline.

Pierson's proposals concerning teaching were congruent with these and, like Gordon and Howell (1959, pp. 384-385), he saw a need for more faculty drawn from the underlying scientific disciplines. "The program outlined above would require a considerable number of new teachers, probably in part from the behavioral sciences, mathematics, statistics, and other related disciplines" (Pierson, 1959, p. 339).

The authors of the landmark studies championed the scientific culture, and their influence on the character of business education during the last 25 years can hardly be overstated. However, some recent thinkers have championed a humanities-based component in business education.

Writing in the *Harvard Business Review,* Behrman and Levin (associate deans of the business school at the University of North Carolina at Chapel Hill) proposed that business schools should reorient themselves to develop managers who take "a broader, more humanistic view of the corporation" (1984, p. 140). In provocative language, they criticized the business faculty members of the post-Pierson-Gordon-Howell era, "most of whom had never succeeded in business but who could tinker both mathematically and behaviorally with significant problems and who often deluded themselves and others into believing that they had actually found solutions" (1984, p. 141).

Behrman and Levin expressed concern about "the inability of [these] faculties to contribute much to policy issues" (1984, p. 144), and they recommended a change in the focus of the faculties and in the focus of the curricula. "Students," they wrote, "must acquire a sense of the sweep of history, . . . develop a holistic view, . . . learn to humanize the corporation, . . . [and] understand the ethical implications of every management decision they make" (1984, p. 142).

In a paper in the *Journal of Business Ethics,* Hosmer (Professor of Policy and Control at the University of Michigan) referred explicitly to the two cultures. "In prior years there was little that could be said . . . except to admit that . . . one of those cultures was fully represented at many schools of business administration" (1985, p. 21). Now, however, the practitioner-oriented literature, including books like Pascale and Athos' *The Art of Japanese Management* and Peters and Waterman's *In Search of Excellence,* has begun to advocate the importance of such "unscientific" efforts as the development of shared, normative values. "If shared values are important in management," he continued, "and the objective evidence . . . seems to indicate that they are, then it is necessary for business managers to be able to work with values, and determine not only what they are but what they should be" (1985, p. 21).

Peters and Waterman, in fact, were sharply critical of "the numerative, rationalist approach to management [which] dominates in the business schools, . . . [which] seeks detached, analytical justification for all decisions, . . . [and which] has arguably led us seriously astray" (1982, p. 29). They cited former investment banker Michael Thomas, who said that today's MBAs "lack liberal arts literacy . . . need a broader vision, a sense of history, [and] perspectives from literature and art" (1980, p. D2).

To a degree, the sort of change advocated by these authors is occurring. During the past twenty years, themes relating to social policy and the nonmarket environment of business have received increased attention in teaching and research. More notably, perhaps, during that same period the discipline of ethics, which is traditionally based in the humanities, has found growing acceptance in business programs (Hoffman & Moore, 1982; McMahon, 1975; McMahon, 1985).

Two Cultures, Two Philosophies

It seems that the two cultures could complement one another in business education. On the one hand, management science is greatly occupied with discovering and describing the *means* by which business ends are or could be achieved—the technical features, for example, of efficient markets, optimal production processes, suboptimal organizations, or satisfying decision making. On the other hand, the humanities (business ethics in particular) are suited to consider what the *ends* of business ultimately ought to be, in terms of human fulfillment and moral merit.

Economic research, for instance, uses the tools and concepts of science to investigate market dynamics against the background assumption that demand and supply curves are shaped by the preference, or utility, functions of market participants; however, it remains for a complementary and nonscientific discipline to investigate and assess the goodness of particular preference functions and, hence, their worthiness to be satisfied through a market dynamic. In keeping with this account, a fully-rounded "two-cultured" education in business economics could include both (a) a scientific analysis of the technical features and relative efficiencies of particular markets and (b) a humanities-based consideration of why these markets should or should not exist.

Regrettably, there is a compelling reason why we cannot expect such a complementary relationship between the two cultures. The deepest differences between the two cultures are philosophical differences, which propel the cultures in opposite directions—into contrary and, nearer the extremes, mutually exclusive views concerning what counts as a method for increasing knowledge and what counts as an investigable object of study.

In science, the definitive methods for increasing knowledge are empirical and mathematical. Objects of study are characteristically understood as mechanisms, that is, as networks of correlated events which reside in space and time, and which have continuity and intelligibility by virtue of the posited relationship of causes to their effects.

The orientation of the humanities is more difficult to describe. In seeking to advance human knowledge, the far-ranging traditions of literature, art, and speculative philosophy reach beyond the bounds of empirical and mathematical demonstration. Plato, for example, conceived the increase of knowledge, in morality and in other areas, as requiring an awakening, a "remembering," of nonempirical objective truths innate and implicit within us. In literature and in art, Shakespeare's *Hamlet* and Michelangelo's *Pieta* are widely regarded as edifying, evocative works which genuinely increase an appreciator's knowledge of what we human beings are, although they do so through fiction and imaginative depiction—methods which, by the standards of science, adduce no data, perform no tests, and explain nothing.

The humanities' most characteristic object of study is our humanity itself, through all its diverse manifestations. The focus often is on questions which scientific method cannot grasp: questions of why human beings exist, of what purpose they have in life (including business life), of what powers they have to know their own possibilities and to choose freely from among those possibilities, and of what they ought to choose (in enterprise and elsewhere) to fulfill their human purpose.

In method, the humanities are as little disposed to argue from systematically collected data as is science to effect its demonstrations through imaginative depiction. In subject matter, purpose, possibility, and free choice are not easily accessible to practitioners of empirical method and are not the sort of tractable phenomena that lend themselves to being cast as components of a cause and effect mechanism.

What emerges here are two very different visions of the world, with very different foundational assumptions concerning both the nature of the world and how we comprehend this world. What does not emerge is a vision of how the two cultures could operate collaboratively in business education.

The Collision Point: Business Ethics and Behavioral Science

In examining business education, proponents of the sciences and of the humanities are unlikely to be at odds in cases where everyone agrees that the particular objects under study are mathematically modelable, empirically explorable, and mechanistic in nature. For example, the mechanisms often studied by operations research, such as the process of assembling a manufactured product, are not very likely to inspire discord.

However, trouble brews when human nature itself is the object of study. In the business disciplines probably the greatest potential for cultural collision exists between behavioral science (which provides fundamental concepts and methods for the studies of organizational behavior, economics, marketing, decision making, and business policy) and business ethics. Both of these disciplines study human action and human decision making (more broadly, human nature). When these disciplines meet, two of the great sticking points between the two cultures attain full visibility: (a) the nature and supportabillty of moral judgments and (b) the correctness of regarding human beings as mechanisms.

Moral Judgments. The reaction of behavioral scientists, in their capacity as behavioral scientists to the question of the supportability of moral judgments ranges from detachment to derision. Their philosophical standard-bearers are the contemporary empiricists, from the positivists, who held the radical view that moral judgments are literally meaningless (cf. Ayer, 1952, p. 108); to Karl Popper (1959), who saw moral judgments as lacking falsifiability and therefore as falling outside the application of the rules for scientific discovery; to J. L. Mackie (1977), who regarded moral judgments as fictions, albeit useful fictions; and to Gilbert Harmon, whose *The Nature of Morality* (1977) fueled the current debate concerning the contention that moral judgments have no explanatory power.

Moral judgments (e.g., judgments about the goodness of particular business practices, or about what ought to be the moral goal of our whole system of enterprise) cannot be supported or confuted by empirical means. David Hume's watershed observation, made in 1737, that you cannot get a moral "ought" from an empirical "is" still stands (see 1967, p. 469). Hence, the truth or falsity of moral judgments cannot be ascertained scientifically. Indeed, their empiricist theory of knowledge makes it difficult for behavioral scientists to be anything but relativists, conventionalists, or skeptics in their view of moral judgments.

In this stream of thought, the organizational studies of Ackerman and Bauer have made an influential contribution to the detachment of social issue management from the traditional concerns of ethics. In their important book, *Corporate Social Responsiveness: The Modern Dilemma*, they wrote, "The semantics of the term 'social responsibility' fand . . . the notions of intent, good will, sacrifice, and voluntary initiative . . . have become progressively inappropriate as these issues have moved inside the firm" (1976, p. 9).

In explaining the imputed moral aspect of business life, organizational behaviorists, like behavioral scientists generally, in the main attempt to present an empirically supported account of moral belief systems. This means that they scientifically observe and test the conditions of the *occurrence* of moral beliefs within a social system. Sometimes they take the extra step, as did Ackerman and Bauer (1976) and Langton and Lewin (1982), of suggesting organizational designs or business practices which will allow companies to respond and adapt to the moral beliefs of the constituencies on which the businesses depend.

However, never is the direct objective of such scientific inquiry to investigate the *truth or falsity* of moral beliefs.

Said another way, the explicit focus is on reacting to public demands and on developing public policy rather than on the responsibility of business per se. Often, this literature conveys the idea that this focus avoids the quagmire of moral debate and deals concretely with the practical concerns of managers who must get on with doing something. In this spirit, Buchholz, Evans, and Wagley, following the earlier work of Preston and Post (1975), wrote:

> The public policy process is the means by which society as a whole articulates its goals and objectives, and directs and stimulates individuals and organizations to contribute to and cooperate with them. Appropriate guidelines for managerial behavior are to be found in the larger society, not in the personal vision of managers or in the special interests of groups. A business organization should therefore analyze and evaluate pressures and stimuli coming from public policy in the same way it analyzes and evaluates market experience and opportunity (1985, p. 32).

Human Mechanisms. It is not difficult to see that the socially well-managed firm is understood here as a mechanism of response. A humanities-based investigation of the imputed moral aspect of business life is likely to see this as inadequate. "One might be forgiven the hope," wrote Goodpaster and Matthews (Harvard Business School), "that the political process will not substitute for the moral judgment of the citizenry or other components of society such as corporations" (1982, p. 77).

Some management scientists might forgive this hope, but few are likely to share it. Their problem is that a mechanism of response cannot exercise moral judgment. The neoclassical economic vision, so widely assumed in business education, is that the role of the firm and of its management is to serve as the optimal transformer between the factor and product markets. The firm so conceived is a machine, a conduit between two huge sets of householders, and it is driven exclusively by the preference functions of those householders. The firm has no satisfactions, no free initiative, no humanity of its own. From the perspective of science, to construe the firm as a moral agent is to commit the fallacy of anthropomorphism.

The work of management scientists like Ackerman and Buchholz has contributed mightily to our understanding of the organizational structures, programs, and practices for effective social issue management. However, from the humanities, perspective, still missing from public policy analysis and the literature of corporate social responsiveness is an explicit treatment of the fundamental justificatory reasons why business should choose to be socially responsive in the first place—some reasons, that is, why business has a responsibility to respond.

In investigating the moral aspect of business life, the behavioral scientist and humanities-based ethicist begin with different views of the nature of what is to be explained. A behavioral scientist assumes that human beings and human organizations are mechanisms (in the sense stated earlier) and looks for the causes of, the stimuli and external pressures which precede, human states and events. The humanities-based ethicist, in the tradition of Plato, Augustine, or Kant, is more likely to assume that human beings (individually and in organizations) are the responsible authors of their own behaviors (i.e., they are autonomous beings who set goals and act freely). The humanities-based thinker does not seek the causes of behavior, but seeks the freely held good reasons for freely choosing to do this or that.

This is the root of the deep tension, or what C. P. Snow called the "incomprehension and dislike," between the two cultures in business education. Science studies mechanisms, and behavioral science in the main conceives human beings as mechanisms. The tradition of the humanities, and ethics within that tradition, in the main conceives human beings as autonomous agents, beings with free will. There is no middle ground, no room for compromise. There are no free mechanisms. An act of free will is gibberish from the perspective of behavioral science: it is, as B. F. Skinner (1971) saw only too clearly, an event without a cause or, perhaps worse, an event which causes itself. From a traditional religious perspective, free will is an important respect in which we human beings were made in the image of God. In this view, we, like god, have the power to create something ex nihilo (out of nothing). Not an entire universe, to be sure, but an entire act of will. However, something from nothing is that most unwanted of developments for the scientist—an utterly unaccoutable intrusion poking into the universe, a miracle. Yet that is precisely what autonomous human nature comes down to, and in this regard it is clearly an anti-scientific concept, a concept *destructive* of the very possibility of scientific explanation.

Conclusion

In important respects, Pierson and Gordon and Howell were wrong. What eluded them was the real nature of the humanities, and, hence, the fundamental significance for the study of business of the humanities' long exploration of human and social purpose. Consequently, they made no substantive allowance for the contribution of the humanities to the life of an educated business person.

Further, although it may not have been the intent of Pierson and Gordon and Howell, in the past quarter of a century the implementors of their recommendations sometimes seem to have been guided by a fallacious inference that because scientific methods are useful in the study of business, therefore business ought to be practiced scientifically. The past 25 years of the business academy have been largely a history of science energetically remaking business in its own image. The end-product of business education is now conceived as a kind of manager-technician, who is equipped with all manner of techniques for mastering the uncounted mechanisms comprising the business world.

Today too few of the policy makers, faculty acquirers, and curriculum designers in business schools have the educational background and peer encouragement needed to help them bring in high quality faculty from the humanities and to undertake the sorts of research and curriculum innovations which such faculty could provide. Behavioral science will soon enter its fourth decade of mainstream research and curriculum development in business education, but, for the most part, experiments with mainstream components in, say, the history of business or the philosophy of business remain unattempted.

Business schools are by nature interdisciplinary, and it makes sense that they should provide an opportunity for encounter between the two cultures even though this would be an encounter which leads to no easy harmony. Either human knowledge, human nature, and human organizations are adequately accounted for in empirical and mechanistic terms or they are not. Both views cannot be true. There is no easy method for settling the disagreement between the two cultures because what counts as an adequate method for arriving at the knowledge needed to resolve the dispute is itself at issue in the dispute. Further, as a practical matter, it is difficult for members of the business academy to focus on these problems, because the fundamental principles governing how one operates in the pursuit of her or his discipline have long since ceased to be issues for most of us.

In the absence of a final resolution, at least one proposal should be made. Business education needs the humanities. As things stand today, the discipline of business ethics is probably the last best hope for the humanities in business education. A primary mission of teachers of business ethics should be to provide a humanities-based counterbalance to the scientific education offered in today's business schools. Business ethics faculty should acquaint their students with humanities-based alternatives to the scientific vision of human knowledge, human nature, and human organizations. They should sensitize their students to the issues that separate the two cultures and to the contribution the humanities can make to questions of human purpose in business. Even if the final answer cannot be delivered, business students deserve the opportunity to become literate in the worldviews of both cultures.

References

Ackerman, R. W., & Bauer, R. A. (1976) *Corporate social responsiveness: The modern dilemma.* Reston, VA: Reston.

Ayer, A. J. (1952) *Language, truth, and logic.* New York: Dover.

Behrman, J. I., & Levin, R. I. (1984) Are business schools doing their job? *Harvard Business Review,* 62(2), 140-47.

Buchholz, R. A., Evans, W. D., & Wagley, R. A. (1985) *Management response to public issues: Concepts and cases in strategy formulation.* Englewood Cliffs, NJ: Prentice-Hall.

Goodpaster, K., & Matthews, J. (1982) Can a corporation have a conscience? *Harvard Business Review,* 60(2), 132-141.

Gordon, R. A., & Howell, J. E. (1959) *Higher education for business.* New York: Columbia University Press.

Harmon, G. (1977) *The nature of morality: An introduction to ethics.* New York: Oxford University Press.

Hoffman, M., & Moore, J. M. (1982) Results of a business ethics curriculum survey conducted by the Center of Business Ethics. *Journal of Business Ethics,* 1, 81 ff.

Hosmer, L. T. (1985) The other 338: Why a majority of our schools of business administration do not offer a course in business ethics. *Journal of Business Ethics,* 4, 17-22.

Hume, D. (1967) *A treatise of human nature.* (L. A. Selby-Bigge, Ed.). London: Oxford University Press. (Original work published in 1737.)

Langton, J. F., & Lewin, A. Y. (1982) Dinosaurs did not survive. *Enterprise,* 1(2), 14-19.

Mackie, J. L. (1977) *Ethics: Inventing right and wrong.* New York: Penguin.

McMahon, T. F. (1975) *Reports on the teaching of socio-ethical issues in collegiate schools of business/public administration.* Charlottesville, VA: Center for the Study of Applied Ethics, The Colgate Darden Graduate School of Business Administration, University of Virginia.

McMahon, T. F. (1985) Socio-ethical issues: Two conceptual frameworks. In P. Werhane & K. D'Andrade (Eds.), *Profit and responsibility: The state of ethics in business.* Lewiston, NY: Edwin Mellen Press.

Peters, T. J., & Waterman, R. H. (1982) *In search of excellence: Lessons from America's best run companies.* New York: Harper & Row.

Pierson, F. C., & Others (1959) *The education of American businessmen.* New York: McGraw-Hill.

Popper, K. R. (1959) *The logic of scientific discovery.* New York: Harper Torchbooks.

Preston, L. E., & Post, J. E. (1975) *Private management and public policy.* Englewood Cliffs, NJ: Prentice-Hall.

Skinner, B. F. (1971) *Beyond freedom and dignity.* New York: Bantam/Vintage.

Snow, C. P. (1956, October 6) The two cultures. *New Statesman & Nation*, pp. 413-414.

Thomas M. (1980, August 21) Businessmen's shortcomings. *New York Times*, p. D2.

PART 5
THE IMPERATIVES
OF VALUES
AND ETHICS

Leadership can have good or bad outcomes. History cites many leaders who wreaked havoc on the world. We could even classify those leaders as successful in that they accomplished their stated goals and fulfilled their visions. Yet, when we think about leadership development, we normally assume a degree of goodness. We want our leaders to make the world a better place in which to live.

There is more to leadership than personal characteristics and organizational needs. What a leader does is not independent of his or her rationale for it. The method or style will often reflect that rationale but not always. As an intellectual process (influence), leadership is not fully revealed. All of the vision may not be shared; the leader helps to co-create a vision with the organization members that may be different from his or her own. A leader may pose as participative but act without regard to the inputs of others. In extreme cases, the leader may tightly control resources to manipulate the people in the organization.

What leaders do may or may not reflect the goals of their organizations. Some have a personal agenda, and the organization is a platform for them to advance their own cause. They use the organization to accomplish individual objectives. Or, they try to reform the organization to fit themselves—a personality cult perhaps. It is important to study the relationship between the organization and leader to see if they are on the same track.

Throughout this book we have used the phrase "successful leadership." Inherent in this is the congruence between the values of the leader and those being led. We are assuming a *shared* set of values. From that, there are ethical standards of behavior that involve a high level of mutual trust between the leader and others in the organization.

The Leader's Responsibility

Shaping the organizational value system is often left to the leader. Through the process of co-creation, everyone shares their personal values; they learn about each other. Hopefully, this communication leads to understanding, acceptance, and trust. The resulting vision represents a collective view and facilitates the action plan to achieve the shared goals.

Once the value system is identified, the leader has the responsibility of incorporating it into the "story" that he or she tells. Plans and programs are framed. People within and outside are made aware of the corporate values. We are talking about such things as "customer first," "integrity," and "service to humankind." These are not mere slogans; they are the standards by which decisions are made and priorities are established. As a total image, the corporate culture is a reflection of those values and people's beliefs in them.

The leader must continually reinforce the values. In speeches, memos, and discussions, organizational values must be repeated. Most importantly, he or she must relate key decisions to the value system in a systematic way. It is one thing to talk about values. The proof is in how we act. People respond to what they see happening around them. If managers are evaluated in terms of how the service people can cut costs (minimizing the time and task), "customer first" may be replaced by the value of "cost first." In fact, this is exactly the dilemma faced when trying to maximize short-run gains at the expense of the long run.

When the value system is breached, the leader must apply the appropriate sanctions. That is the *only* way that the leader can effectively reinforce corporate values. "Gray areas" or "just this once" are excuses for abandoning values. When a salesperson misrepresents the product, "integrity" is no longer relevant *unless* everyone sees that such behavior will not be tolerated.

Ethical Standards

There are, then, acceptable and unacceptable behaviors. Some organizations attempt to specify these in policies and procedures. The problem here is that covering the range of all possible behaviors is almost impossible. Rules are to be followed, but we also need to establish an inherent sense of what is "right" so that everyone has confidence in their actions. We want people to act in the appropriate ways because they personally believe in a shared set of values. Then, the behaviors reflect an emotional tie as well as a procedural correctness.

Many organizations and professions have adopted codes of ethics. These formal statements of expected behavior do not always reflect the beliefs of everyone within the organization or profession. The effectiveness of such codes depends in large part on the leader. Once again, actions must be evaluated in terms of the ethical standards; sanctions must be applied to individuals who violate the code. A formal statement has no meaning unless it actually reflects behaviors.

More than tacit compliance with standards of conduct is necessary if an organization is to consider itself ethical. All members must accept the organization's standards and values if they are truly committed to ethical (and not simply legal) conduct.

Thus, reinforcement is necessary to remind people of our values and to remind us of the reason for ethical actions. If we truly understand, we will incorporate those values into our personal lives or leave the organization. Our goal, then, is to make the employee a stakeholder so that the personal value system is consistent with the values and ethics of the organization. This is a challenge for leadership.

Leadership Perspectives

Does the leader bring a value set to the organization, or does he or she help to build shared values? Probably both. This process of establishing values is really the essence of corporate culture. Just as our society represents a variety of ethnic cultures (each with a unique set of values), organizations include people with a variety of outlooks. The leader is a social architect who builds a culture that represents the unique properties of the organization *and* allows each individual to accept those values as a part of his or her own.

Standards of behavior—ethics—then emerge. From the top down, the leader must continually reinforce the values and ethical behaviors. Noncompliance must be dealt with in an uncompromising way. While the leader cannot physically be everywhere at once, his or her philosophy and values concerning "how we do things around here" can be.

In his article "Shaping Business Values," Thomas Horton sets out the process by which the leader shapes the values of an organization. This brief, straightforward approach is an excellent guide. Horton's charge is relevant to both the public and private sectors.

Sir Adrian Cadbury takes a very unique approach in "Ethical Managers Make Their Own Rules." He links society to organizations and recognizes that we must have clear direction from the larger society before we can expect organization leaders to make consistent, ethical decisions. However, Cadbury does note that once societal values are made clear, the responsibility for ethical standards conforming to those values rests with leadership.

In "The Hollow Executive," Robert Gilbreath notes that corporations don't set (or apply) ethical standards. People do. Leaders empower everyone in the organization to expect ethical behavior through a sense of self—a "New Age," wholistic approach. Gilbreath makes the leader ultimately accountable, but he also stresses the importance of shared rules.

When all is said and done, it is the leader who keeps the organization together. Vision provides direction. Sharing responsibility creates ownership among organization members. The leader's example of hard work and commitment helps to create an environment of trust and loyalty. Confident decisions come from self-knowledge. But the glue that holds it all together is the corporate culture—a shared set of values that is reflected in consistent and equitable standards of ethical behavior.

17
SHAPING BUSINESS VALUES

Thomas R. Horton

Closely knit members of an organization are sometimes referred to as a "team." On a broader scale, some companies see their employees as a kind of "family." The implication in the use of these terms is that there are shared values at work, people pulling together in the same direction.

This sense of belonging is a strong asset. Any group endeavor is best accomplished when there is a commonality of purpose, a shared sense of wanting to succeed together, a belongingness, so to speak. But this idea does not develop automatically. On the contrary, many organizations are highly segmented by walls of misunderstanding between geographical, divisional, or departmental units. Under these conditions, damaging intramural rivalries are inevitable.

In a business organization, the responsibility for instilling the sense of community capable of overriding these divisive forces rests with the CEO in situations involving the entire company or major subunits. In other circumstances, a lower unit leader may hold the best position for initiating action to unify his or her resources. But whatever the focus of responsibility to take action, the true business leader must be one who is capable of inspiring and changing others, and who can engage the will and efforts of the staff in the pursuit of a common cause.

This, of course, is no snap assignment. A personal and deep commitment must be given to the values the leader wants the organization to adopt, and he or she must be a living example, a person who makes such values evident in every action. It goes without saying that such actions must be consistent with the values and beliefs communicated by the leader. Any inconsistency between what the leader says and does can damage his or her credibility and the entire organization's value system. For example, the chief executive who criticizes workaholics and encourages his staff to take adequate vacations sabotages credibility if he constantly telephones people on weekends demanding instantaneous action or information. A CEO who preaches on the need for highly ethical behavior but uses company resources for wholly personal purposes surely stands out as a hypocrite. Such contradictory behavior is certain to deafen others in the organization to what the chief says.

The values and beliefs that help shape the behavior of employees represent a large part of what we call corporate culture. In recent years much has been written about corporate culture, and the many articles dealing with Japanese management have encouraged some organizations to copy, rather haphazardly, various "Japanese" techniques, such as quality circles. Later writings that have described successful U.S.-based companies have apparently caused other company presidents to believe that they can attain similar success merely by imitating their behavioral characteristics. But that's not necessarily so, as indicated by a recent report of what happened when a high-level executive tried to impose the cultural values described in such a book on a major unit of a traditionally rigid firm. Though his efforts yielded positive results, he was ousted from his position because he had tried to overlay a different set of values on a deeply ingrained culture, and they simply did not fit. Values must be developed from within.

It is certainly true, however, that the most successful organizations—including some that have been described in recent best-selling books—are those that have been fundamentally committed to a set of solid values. One well-known technological firm, a leader in its field, has been guided for 60 years by its founder's unshakable belief in (1) respect for the individual employee, (2) the value of customer service, and (3) the importance of ethical behavior. Another firm—respected throughout industry for its marketing prowess—has been equally dedicated to product quality. In still another instance, a firm's founder has sought to instill in her people her unbounded self-confidence—an important value in a door-to-door sales operation. The values that guide each of these organizations are understood by their employees, and the leader has a responsibility for insuring that the particular beliefs or set of values survives.

The real leader brings his whole being—cultural and civic, as well as business—and his whole understanding to the workplace. At times this may manifest itself through involvement in the local board of education, commitment to the arts, or support of some important civic cause. By example, he may suggest that a businessperson will be more successful if his or her perspective is broad and interests are varied. An effective leader generally has widespread interests, is a reader and thinker, and, like Henry Adams' great teacher, "can never tell where his influence stops."

The chief executive officer of the corporation for which I worked as a young manager had strong beliefs, including one that centered on the importance of the individual and the need to develop the potential of employees. On one occasion I embarrassed myself greatly by using poor judgment at a meeting at which the CEO was present. When the meeting ended, he interrupted his schedule to take me aside and explain in private what I had done wrong, and then offered to help "get me tuned up." He also took time on several later occasions to do just that, an effort for which I have ever since been grateful. He put much energy into demonstrating his personal convictions.

To create deeply held values within the organization, one must proceed deliberately, and the starting place is one's own personal value system. I recommend the following steps:

- *Make sure your personal value system is well formulated and internally consistent.* Determine which values and beliefs are appropriate to try to instill in others and which are not. Observe carefully what values or beliefs your company currently seems to demonstrate, and determine which are positive but in need of enhancement and which may be causing negative effects.
- *On the basis of this assessment, define the values that you consider basic, to the success of your company in the future.* Don't let the exercise become too ambitious or complicated; select only those values that can be soundly justified and clearly articulated.
- *Make certain those who report directly to you understand your objectives;* it's important that all key managers buy into the effort to instill these beliefs and, for that matter, try to improve them. Unless they share ownership of the effort, it is unlikely to be successful.
- *Articulate the company's basic values through direct or spoken communication with all employees.* Roam the ship, talking and listening to peers, employees, and supervisors at all levels, testing out ideas in brief discussions in language that is straightforward and direct.
- *Reward adequately those whose achievements have resulted from value-driven efforts.* Highlight these accomplishments as examples for all.
- *Be as dramatic as possible in underlining the importance placed on the basic values.* Announcements at employee meetings and in promotional material should be as explicit as possible to foster full understanding.

■ *Have the performance of the company or work unit evaluated.* One approach is an anonymous upward communication program that encourages employees to voice their concerns about perceived inconsistencies between values and actions.

The leadership style outlined here demands wholehearted commitment; it calls for careful thought, almost limitless energy, and unswerving vigilance. But the benefits are well worth the effort, and then some.

A company that spotlights its fundamental values and wins support for them gains higher levels of cooperation, develops greater cohesion, and builds a solid foundation for moving ahead. Employees also gain; they win a greater opportunity for personal fulfillment because they are assured that, by taking actions that conform to fundamental values shared by peers and their organizational leaders, they are contributing directly to both individual and company success. Common values—and broad-based commitment to them—are matchless incentives to superior performance.

18
ETHICAL MANAGERS MAKE THEIR OWN RULES

Sir Adrian Cadbury

In 1900 Queen Victoria sent a decorative tin with a bar of chocolate inside to all of her soldiers who were serving in South Africa. These tins still turn up today, often complete with their contents, a tribute to the collecting instinct. At the time, the order faced my grandfather with an ethical dilemma. He owned and ran the second-largest chocolate company in Britain, so he was trying harder and the order meant additional work for the factory. Yet he was deeply and publicly opposed to the Anglo-Boer War. He resolved the dilemma by accepting the order, but carrying it out at cost. He therefore made no profit out of what he saw as an unjust war, his employees benefited from the additional work, the soldiers received their royal present, and I am still sent the tins.

My grandfather was able to resolve the conflict between the decision best for his business and his personal code of ethics because he and his family owned the firm which bore their name. Certainly his dilemma would have been more acute if he had had to take into account the interests of outside shareholders, many of whom would no doubt have been in favor both of the war and of profiting from it. But even so, not all my grandfather's ethical dilemmas could be as straightforwardly resolved.

So strongly did my grandfather feel about the South African War that he acquired and financed the only British newspaper which opposed it. He was also against gambling, however, and so he tried to run the paper without any references to horse racing. The effect on the newspaper's circulation was such that he had to choose between his ethical beliefs. He decided, in the end, that it was more important that the paper's voice be heard as widely as possible than that gambling should thereby receive some mild encouragement. The decision was doubtless a relief to those working on the paper and to its readers.

The way my grandfather settled these two clashes of principle brings out some practical points about ethics and business decisions. In the first place, the possibility that ethical and commercial considerations will conflict has always faced those who run companies. It is not a new problem. The difference now is that a more widespread and critical interest is being taken in our decisions and in the ethical judgments which lie behind them.

Secondly, as the newspaper example demonstrates, ethical signposts do not always point in the same direction. My grandfather had to choose between opposing a war and condoning gambling. The rule that it is best to tell the truth often runs up against the rule that we should not hurt people's feelings unnecessarily. There is no simple, universal formula for solving ethical problems. We have to choose from our own codes of conduct whichever rules are appropriate to the case in hand; the outcome of those choices makes us who we are.

Lastly, while it is hard enough to resolve dilemmas when our personal rules of conduct conflict, the real difficulties arise when we have to make decisions which affect the interests of others. We can work out what weighting to give to our own rules through trial and error. But business decisions require us to do the same for others by allocating weights to all the conflicting interests which may be involved. Frequently, for example, we must balance the interests of employment against those of shareholders. But even that sounds more straightforward than it really is, because there may well be differing views among the shareholders, and the interests of past, present, and future employees are unlikely to be identical.

Eliminating ethical considerations from business decisions would simplify the management task, and Milton Friedman has urged something of the kind in arguing that the interaction between business and society should be left to the political process. "Few trends could so thoroughly undermine the very foundation of our free society," he writes in *Capitalism and Freedom*, "as the acceptance by corporate officials of a social responsibility other than to make as much money for their shareholders as possible."

But the simplicity of this approach is deceptive. Business is part of the social system and we cannot isolate the economic elements of major decisions from their social consequences. So there are no simple rules.

Those who make business decisions have to assess the economic and social consequences of their actions as best as they can and come to their conclusions on limited information and in a limited time.

We Judge Companies—and Managers—by Their Actions, Not Their Pious Statements of Intent

As will already be apparent, I use the word ethics to mean the guidelines or rules of conduct by which we aim to live. It is, of course, foolhardy to write about ethics at all, because you lay yourself open to the charge of taking up a position of moral superiority, of failing to practice what you preach, or both. I am not in a position to preach nor am I promoting a specific code of conduct. I believe, however, that it is useful to all of us who are responsible for business decisions to acknowledge the part which ethics plays in those decisions and to encourage discussion of how best to combine commercial and ethical judgments. Most business decisions involve some degree of ethical judgment; few can be taken solely on the basis of arithmetic.

While we refer to a company as having a set of standards, that is a convenient shorthand. The people who make up the company are responsible for its conduct and it is their collective actions which determine the company's standards. The ethical standards of a company are judged by its actions, not by pious statements of intent put out in its name. This does not mean that those who head companies should not set down what they believe their companies stand for—hard though that is to do. The character of a company is a matter of importance to those in it, to those who do business with it, and to those who are considering joining it.

What matters most, however, is where we stand as individual managers and how we behave when faced with decisions which require us to combine ethical and commercial judgments. In approaching such decisions, I believe it is helpful to go through two steps. The first is to determine, as precisely as we can, what our personal rules of conduct are. This does not mean drawing up a list of virtuous notions, which will probably end up as a watered-down version of the Scriptures without their literary merit. It does mean looking back at decisions we have made and working out from there what our rules actually are. The aim is to avoid confusing ourselves and everyone else by declaring one set of principles and acting on another. Our ethics are expressed in our.actions, which is why they are usually clearer to others than to ourselves.

Once we know where we stand personally we can move on to the second step, which is to think through who else will be affected by the decision and how we should weight their interest in it. Some interests will be represented by well-organized groups; others will have no one to put their case. If a factory manager is negotiating a wage claim with employee representatives, their remit is to look after the interests of those who are already employed. Yet the effect of the wage settlement on the factory's costs may well determine whether new employees are likely to be taken on. So the manager cannot ignore the interest of potential employees in the outcome of the negotiation, even though that interest is not represented at the bargaining table.

Black and White Alternatives Are a Regrettable Sign of the Times

The rise of organized interest groups makes it doubly important that managers consider the arguments of everyone with a legitimate interest in a decision's outcome. Interest groups seek publicity to promote their causes and they have the advantage of being single-minded: they are against building an airport on a certain site, for example, but take no responsibility for finding a better alternative. This narrow focus gives pressure groups a debating advantage against managements, which cannot evade the responsibility for taking decisions in the same way.

In *The Hard Problems of Management*, Mark Pastin has perceptively referred to this phenomenon as the ethical superiority of the uninvolved, and there is a good deal of it about. Pressure groups are skilled at seizing the high moral ground and arguing that our judgment as managers is at best biased and at worst influenced solely by private gain because we have a direct commercial interest in the outcome of our decisions. But as managers we are also responsible for arriving at business decisions which take account of all the interests concerned; the uninvolved are not.

At times the campaign to persuade companies to divest themselves of their South African subsidiaries has exemplified this kind of ethical high-handedness. Apartheid is abhorrent politically, socially, and morally. Those who argue that they can exert some influence on the direction of change by staying put believe this as sincerely as those who favor divestment. Yet many anti-apartheid campaigners reject the proposition that both sides have the same end in view. From their perspective it is self-evident that the only ethical course of action is for companies to wash their hands of the problems of South Africa by selling out.

Managers cannot be so self-assured. In deciding what weight to give to the arguments for and against divestment, we must consider who has what at stake in the outcome of the decision. The employees of a South African subsidiary have the most direct stake, as the decision affects their future; they are also the group whose voice is least likely to be heard outside South Africa. The shareholders have at stake any loss on divestment, against which must be balanced any gain in the value of their shares through severing the South African connection. The divestment lobby is the one group for whom the decision is costless eithe: way.

What is clear even from this limited analysis is that there is no general answer to the question of whether companies should sell their South African subsidiaries or not. Pressure to reduce complicated issues to straightforward alternatives, one of which is right and other wrong, is a regrettable sign of the times. But boards are rarely presented with two clearly opposed alternatives. Companies faced with the same issues will therefore properly come to different conclusions and their decisions may alter over time.

A less contentious divestment decision faced my own company when we decided to sell our foods division. Because the division was mainly a U.K. business with regional brands, it did not fit the company's strategy, which called for concentrating resources behind our confectionery and soft drinks brands internationally. But it was an attractive business in it's own right and the decision to sell prompted both a management bid and external offers.

Employees working in the division strongly supported the management bid and made their views felt. In this instance, they were the best organized interest group and they had more information available to them to back their case than any of the other parties involved. What they had at stake was also very clear.

From the shareholders' point of view the premium over asset value offered by the various bidders was a key aspect of the decision. They also had an interest in seeing the deal completed without regulatory delays and without diverting too much management attention from the ongoing business. In addition, the way in which the successful bidder would guard the brand name had to considered, since the division would take with it products carrying the parent company's name.

In weighing the advantages and disadvantages of the various offers, the board considered all the groups, consumers among them, who would be affected by the sale. But our main task was to reconcile the interests of the employees and of the shareholders. (The more, of course, we can encourage employees to become shareholders, the closer together the interests of these two stakeholders will be brought.) The division's management upped its bid in the face of outside competition, and after due deliberation we decided to sell to the management team, believing that this choice best balanced the diverse interests at stake.

Actions Are Unethical If They Won't Stand Scrutiny

Companies whose activities are international face an additional complication in taking their decisions. They aim to work to the same standards of business conduct wherever they are and to behave as good corporate citizens of the countries in which they trade. But the two aims are not always compatible; promotion on merit may be the rule of the company and promotion by seniority the custom of the country. In addition, while the financial arithmetic on which companies base their decisions is generally accepted, what is considered ethical varies among cultures.

If what would be considered corruption in the company's home territory is an accepted business practice elsewhere, how are local managers expected to act? Companies could do business only in countries in which they feel ethically at home, provided always that their shareholders take the same view. But this approach could prove unduly restrictive, and there is also a certain arrogance in dismissing foreign codes of conduct without considering why they may be different. If companies find, for example, that they have to pay customs officers in another country just to do their job, it may be that the state is simply transferring its responsibilities to the private sector as an alternative to using taxation less efficiently to the same end.

Nevertheless, this example brings us to one of the most common ethical issues companies face—how far to go in buying business? What payments are legitimate for companies to make to win orders and, the reverse side of that coin, when do gifts to employees become bribes? I use two rules of thumb to test whether a payment is acceptable from the company's point of view: Is the payment on the face of the invoice? Would it embarrass the recipient to have the gift mentioned in the company newspaper?

The first test ensures that all payments, however unusual they may seem, are recorded and go through the books. The second is aimed at distinguishing bribes from gifts, a definition which depends on the size of the gift and the influence it is likely to have on the recipient. The value of a case of whiskey to me would be limited, because I only take it as medicine. We know ourselves whether a gift is acceptable or not and we know that others will know if they are aware of the nature of the gift.

As for payment on the face of the invoice, I have found it a useful general rule precisely because codes of conduct do vary round the world. It has legitimized some otherwise unlikely company payments, to the police in one country, for example, and to the official planning authorities in another, but all went through the books and were audited. Listing a payment on the face of the invoice may not be a sufficient ethical test, but it is a necessary one; payments outside the company's system are corrupt and corrupting.

The logic behind these rules of thumb is that openness and ethics go together and that actions are unethical if they will not stand scrutiny. Openness in arriving at decisions reflects the same logic. It gives those with an interest in a particular decision the chance to make their views known and opens to argument the basis on which the decision is finally taken. This in turn enables the decision makers to learn from experience and to improve their powers of judgment.

Openness is also, I believe, the best way to disarm outside suspicion of companies' motives and actions. Disclosure is not a panacea for improving the relations between business and society, but the willingness to operate an open system is the foundation of those relations. Business needs to be open to the views of society and open in return about its own activities; this is essential for the establishment of trust.

For the same reasons, as managers we need to be candid when making decisions about other people. Dr. Johnson reminds us that when it comes to lapidary inscriptions, "no man is upon oath." But what should be disclosed in references, in fairness to those looking for work and to those who are considering employing them?

The simplest rule would seem to be that we should write the kind of reference we would wish to read. Yet "do as you would be done by" says nothing about ethics. The actions which result from applying it could be ethical or unethical, depending on the standards of the initiator. The rule could be adapted to help managers determine their ethical standards, however, by reframing it as a question: If you did business with yourself, how ethical would you think you were?

Anonymous letters accusing an employee of doing something discreditable create another context in which candor is the wisest course. Such letters cannot by definition be answered, but they convey a message to those who receive them, however warped or unfair the message may be. I normally destroy these letters, but tell the person concerned what has been said. This conveys the disregard I attach to nameless allegation, but preserves the rule of openness. From a practical point of view, it serves as a warning if there is anything in the allegations; from an ethical point of view, the degree to which my judgment of the person may now be prejudiced is known between us.

Shelving Hard Decisions Is the Least Ethical Course

The last aspect of ethics in business decisions I want to discuss concerns our responsibility for the level of employment; what can or should companies do about the provision of jobs? This issue is of immediate concern to European managers because unemployment is higher in Europe than it is in the United States and the net number of new jobs created has been much lower. It comes to the fore whenever companies face decisions which require a trade-off between increasing efficiency and reducing numbers employed.

If you believe, as I do, that the primary purpose of a company is to satisfy the needs of its customers and to do so profitably, the creation of jobs cannot be the company's goal as well. Satisfying customers requires companies to compete in the marketplace, and so we cannot opt out of introducing new technology, for example, to preserve jobs. To do so would be to deny consumers the benefits of progress, to shortchange the shareholders, and in the longer run to put the jobs of everyone in the company at risk. What destroys jobs certainly and permanently is the failure to be competitive.

Experience says that the introduction of new technology creates more jobs than it eliminates, in ways which cannot be forecast. It may do so, however, only after a time lag, and those displaced may not, through lack of skills, be able to take advantage of the new opportunities when they arise. Nevertheless, the company's prime responsibility to everyone who has a stake in it is to retain its competitive edge, even if this means a loss of jobs in the short run.

Where companies do have a social responsibility, however, is in how we manage that situation, how we smooth the path of technological change. Companies are responsible for the timing of such changes and we are in a position to involve those who will be affected by the way in which those changes are introduced. We also have a vital resource in our capacity to provide training, so that continuing employees can take advantage of change and those who may lose their jobs can more readily find new ones.

In the United Kingdom, an organization called Business in the Community has been established to encourage the formation of new enterprises. Companies have backed it with cash and with secondments. The secondment of able managers to worthwhile institutions is a particularly effective expression of concern, because the ability to manage is such a scarce resource. Through Business in the Community we can create jobs collectively, even if we cannot do so individually, and it is clearly in our interest to improve the economic and social climate in this way.

Throughout, I have been writing about the responsibilities of those who head companies and my emphasis has been on taking decisions, because that is what directors and managers are appointed to do. What concerns me is that too often the public pressures which are put on companies in the name of ethics encourage their boards to put off decisions or to wash their hands of problems. There may well be commercial reasons for those choices, but there are rarely ethical ones. The ethical bases on which decisions are arrived at will vary among companies, but shelving those decisions is likely to be the least ethical course.

The company which takes drastic action in order to survive is more likely to be criticized publicly than the one which fails to grasp the nettle and gradually but inexorably declines. There is always a temptation to postpone difficult decisions, but it is not in society's interests that hard choices should be evaded because of public clamor or the possibility of legal action. Companies need to be encouraged to take the decisions which face them; the responsibility for providing that encouragement rests with society as a whole.

Society sets the ethical framework within which those who run companies have to work out their own codes of conduct. Responsibility for decisions, therefore, runs both ways. Business has to take account of its responsibilities to society in coming to its decisions, but society has to accept its responsibilities for setting the standards against which those decisions are made.

19
THE HOLLOW EXECUTIVE

Robert D. Gilbreath

That business ethics is a compelling and especially topical subject demands little reinforcement. The press abounds with accounts of insider trading scandals, check kiting schemes, money laundering, and questionable contracting practices. Fortune 500 companies compose ethical codes, and university business schools squeeze ethics "modules" into their curricula.

These headlines, of course, represent only the tip of the iceberg. As corporate America struggles in a business environment that grows increasingly complex, managers are confronted with a rapidly expanding list of ethical questions that defy easy solutions. Should a company "absorb" new technology presented by a potential supplier who ultimately loses a bid to do business? What ethical responsibilities must a multinational corporation assume in a host country? Should the managers of a foreign subsidiary compromise their code of ethics to adapt to a new business environment? How does a manager balance the needs of his company with those of a loyal employee who suddenly develops a case of chronic absenteeism?

Breaking a Pattern
Considering the variety and abundance of the headlines, and assuming that what reaches public scrutiny represents only a fraction of what occurs, the compelling question is not whether one occurrence is more or less ethical than another, but whether a pattern exists. I think one does, and it concerns not merely the practices of corporations or highly visible executives but individual choices and courses of action taken at all levels.

Reprinted by permission from *New Management* 4:4 (Spring 1987), pp. 24-28. Copyright 1987 by John Wiley & Sons, Inc. All rights reserved.

Corporations do not set or apply ethical standards, people do, and because our society has enforced a value-free business environment for so long, our executive ranks are being filled by value-less members, men and women who are not *un*ethical in the literal sense of acting against ethical standards but characteristically *non*ethical. They are without ethics, hollow. The Hollow Executive has no supporting framework, no context of values. And without a framework he cannot support or maintain individual content, a sense of self.

If we are to convert the Hollow Executive we must first understand why ethics are increasingly vital to corporate survival. Here are some of the most important reasons.

The easy decisions have already been made. Cost cutting, layoffs, and reorganizations have been relentless, but the next series of transactions will involve harder choices, choices that will crowd the borders between economic and ethical issues.

All business is public business. What used to be private affairs between buyer and seller are now open to the world. Every business decision sooner or later will occur in a fishbowl.

Management prudence is the new standard. Audits, reviews, and second guessing are facts of contemporary business. Questions are moving from governance to prudence, and prudence implies ethics.

The list of stakeholders is growing. Customers and owners have been joined by other groups such as the press and various consumer organizations, which are often demanding, insistent, and powerful.

The hero is vulnerable. Business heroes have been basking in the spotlight of public enchantment, but it won't take long for that light to turn to heat. Imperfections will show, and vulnerability will increase.

Scapegoats are needed. More business failures and greater losses create a need for specific scapegoats. It is much easier to target individuals and a lack of ethics than complex economic decisions as the reasons why something went wrong.

Traditional values are coming back. With the New Age paradigm emerging in our society, traditional values are resurfacing in a fresh way. Holism, systems thinking, and the integration of once-separate disciplines—knowledge and work—characterize this new era. The distinction between what is intelligent or economically sound and what is "good" is evaporating.

The Contemporary Caricature

With New Age views comes a need to resurrect or redefine the business angst that has nettled societies since the beginning of the Industrial Revolution. In the 1940s business alienation was personified by

Willy Loman in *Death of a Salesman*. In the 1950s and 1960s we read of *The Man in the Gray Flannel Suit* and *The Organization Man*, characters with cartoon proportions whom we nonetheless dreaded becoming.

The Organization Man saw his identify as one and the same with his corporation. He projected himself into the corporate matrix of values; he became "It." The Man in the Gray Flannel Suit projected himself into the herd, embracing conformity; he became "Them."

Today's caricature is quite different. The Hollow Executive doesn't borrow an ethical framework from a company or a crowd; he simply goes without one. He is much more difficult to spot and transform into a cartoon character, because without an ethical framework and an individual identity, he becomes today's "Invisible Man."

Philosophy of Grab

We know the Hollow Executive not by his shape or content but only by his tracks. We see these tracks wandering throughout a business career because they follow no map, set no pattern, nor obey any logic save a constant need to decide and act upon what seems to be his self-interest. If he has a philosophy it is only in the most perverse sense, the "philosophy of grab."

Hollow Executives vary. Some are fairly predictable because they frame each decision against immediate self-interest. (What's in this for me, now?) More sophisticated types take a longer-range view. (What's in this for me as part of my personal advancement, today, and perhaps in the future?) In either case, Hollow Executives suffer tremendously. They worry, plot endlessly, and confront anxiety much more frequently because they must make each decision on its own merits, without an ethical framework. They can rely only on the comfort of their individual cunning, their craftiness over time.

Self-interest for the Self-interested

Hollow Executives are inwardly motivated and propelled to success with the burning engine of self-interest. But this very engine can be harnessed to meet the ethical tests of the New Age. Perhaps we can show the Hollow Executive that an underlying fabric of sustained values is, in fact, in his self-interest. We start by showing how ethics support a simple yet demanding function of management: decision making.

Most successful corporations have discovered that decision making is most effective when supported by a strategy. Each choice is tested by asking: Does it contribute to the overriding strategy? The same is true for the individual decision maker, today's executive. An ethical framework is no more than a personal strategy in this regard. Countless unnecessary questions about a decision's immediate and ultimate consequences can be avoided by testing each alternative this way: Does it fit my ethical framework?

Ethical criteria are simple yet elegant. And as with literature, art, or any other form of expression, elegance transcends time much better than complexity or intricacy. Ethics apply across the space and time of our business careers. Craftiness is much more difficult to sustain; it requires too much too often, and it gives too little comfort in return.

The Ultimate Pragmatist's Tool

An ethical framework makes many decisions straightforward and easier to face. But there are other reasons why such a framework is in our self-interest.

Ethics build consistency. Our choices and their outcomes are recognizable, fairly predictable, and, therefore, justifiable. We are stable, sustainable and forthright, attractive features for anyone at the helm of any business.

Ethics instill confidence. We face uncertain and often turbulent times ahead. An ethical framework allows us to attack uncertainty with the confidence that, regardless of what contests we confront, there is a set of guiding principles to sustain us.

Ethics moderate competitive stress. As noted psychologist Nathaniel Branden says, "Genuine self-esteem is not competitive or comparative." An ethical framework helps to define us, to give us the self-esteem that is so desperately needed in a world of alienation where loss of identity is the greatest loss of all. We compare ourselves against our ethical standards, not against the corporation of the herd.

Ethics help build teams. When our ethical context is apparent to others, they can readily decide whether to join our efforts. Values are understood, relationships take shape, and mutuality of interest is easier to identify and sustain.

Ethics empower others. Changing business goals, technologies, markets, and social conditions form the backdrop of contemporary management. To manage in flux we must develop adaptive procedures and abandon "rule by rote." We cannot hard-wire the decisions of subordinates in order to assure performance. We now need trust. And trust, either upward or downward, is difficult for the Hollow Executive to purchase.

Ethics promote "value proximity." The term "management proximity" describes the intimacy or closeness between a manager and the object of his effort. That closeness is essential if the executive is to remain a participant in company processes.

Value proximity is an intimacy between the business leader and those under his command or influence. With proximate values (only achievable with an ethical framework) the executive moves even closer to "the managed," whether it is a corporation, market, project, or product. With a high level of value proximity, a large amount of explanation, ordering, rewarding, punishing, and persuasion becomes superfluous.

A sustained set of ethical principles, then, becomes the goal not only of those executives who want to be "right" but of those who want to be successful. Even skeptics, the business pragmatists, must enter the New Age. Even they must now recognize ethics as the ultimate pragmatist's power tool.

The Mart of Economic Strife and Gain

Ethical fabrics serve us, comfort us in times of turbulence, and empower the management function. Are they enough to fill the Hollow Executive? No. They provide a necessary framework, a *context* for each of us, but they do not assure the proper *content*. They provide the structure, but not the essence it must contain. For the Hollow Executive to become whole, he must fill the personal vessel with a sense of self, a priceless identity.

Since ethics is that body of philosophy dealing with the study of ideal conduct, it is appropriate to turn to philosophy in pursuing the sense of self. (Here is where New Age management departs from conventional wisdom: we can explore any field, any subject when searching for better ways to conduct a commercial enterprise.)

Old management frameworks held no room for philosophic quests. As Will Durant writes in *The Story of Philosophy,* "There is a pleasure in philosophy, and a lure even in the mirages of metaphysics, which every student feels until the coarse necessities of physical existence drags him from the heights of thought into the mart of economic strife and gain."

Those words were written in 1926, in the days of *Babbitt* and *Main Street*, not in the New Age. When we enter the mart of economic strife today, we must drag philosophy in with us; survival demands no less. And we must ignore no other sources of wisdom. Following the advice of Danish physicist Neils Bohr, executives should "hold no hope for any speculation that does not look absurd at first glance."

Here is such a speculation: The executive who is best suited to the demands of an uncertain future constantly questions his sense of self.

The questioning executive is occupied in the pursuit of a personal identify. The lost executive, the hollow one, does not know such a search is
imperative. Ethics without a sense of self cannot exist.

Destroying a Sense of Self

We need not abandon our identities to be successful, but successful
people often have. Whether by direct attack or benign neglect, the Hollow Executive has certainly abandoned his. Here are some of the ways
in which Hollow Executives destroy their sense of self.

Reduce their sense of self to quantitative measure. They believe they exist
only in the dimensions of measure (profit, sales, organization size) or in
comparison with others or established standards.

Condemn it to competition. Competition with one's potential is healthy.
Negative aspects of competition come about when Hollow Executives
tell people they cannot be different without being better or worse than
others.

Cheapen it through exchange value. They destroy their sense of self
when they define people as marketable commodities. They tell themselves or others that they don't exist save in someone else's value
scheme.

Denigrate their accomplishments. This is the constant "but what have
you done lately?" insistence that dogs even the most prolific achievers.
Continuous, voracious expectations discount or ignore previous accomplishments.

Kill their sense of self by making it a tool. They see individuals as means
and not ends, as links in some big machine called a business. Listen to
the man from the mouse hole in Dostoyevski's *Notes from Underground*:
"I believe this is so and I am prepared to vouch for it, because it seems
to me the meaning of man's life consists in proving to himself every
minute that he is a man and not a piano key."

Encouraging a Sense of Self

We can defend against the daily erosion of self but will still end up
hollow unless we take positive, proactive steps. Considering the relentless attack of destructive agents, we must constantly build to stay
ahead. Here are some steps we can take.

Admit and embrace human qualities and limitations. We must refuse to be
lowered to singular comparisons as we acknowledge our personal,
qualitative, and subjective essence. We should take the gift and glory of
being unique.

Define ourselves without using others. When it comes to human beings, truly objective comparisons cannot be made. We should be able to be with others without measuring ourselves against them.

Resist becoming a marketing package. Salary and perks are often ludicrous. The inventor of the "pet rock" must have grossed more in a year than the President of the United States, but we cannot plan our lives only in terms of accumulated dross. Prostitution in any form is abhorrent most because it converts a human to a salable object.

Revel in accomplishment. We must seize the moment of success in ourselves and others and enjoy it. We should not be embarrassed or modest when it comes to difficulties overcome.

Demand the right to be human. We must allow ourselves to fail, to have emotions, to be indecisive at times. It's OK to admit a sense of wonder or an inability to understand. Far from weaknesses, these are human qualities, rare and to be treasured. They are not possessed by a computer or a piano key.

Trust ourselves. Marilyn Ferguson said it best: "Even more efficient than a police force, it is distrust of self that makes people vulnerable and obedient."

On the Edge of the New Age

Willy Loman, The Man in the Gray Flannel Suit, The Organization Man: these are the zombies that stalked our business past. Each in his own way was lost when it came to content and context. And although we may be on the edge of a New Age of management, a newer, more insidious, character is lurking, sometimes in the guise of perceived power and wealth: the Hollow Executive. He is too elusive to be stereotyped, too crafty to be reduced to cartoon proportions, and too contemporary to be easily dismissed.

If we are to avoid becoming the Hollow Executive, or wish to change should this depiction seem painfully recognizable, we must accept an ethical framework and support it with a dynamic sense of self. These two attributes cannot be separated or stilled. As Erich Fromm tells us, "Use of reason presupposes the sense of self; so does ethical judgment and action." He went further to ask, "How can ethics be a significant part of a life in which the individual becomes an automaton, in which he serves the big It?" The "big It" need not be a corporation. It can be a relentless drive for success.

We now know that ethics, a sense of self, and an ability to empower the values of others are mutually dependent and closely entwined. And we should know that entry to the New Age of management is restricted to those who realize this. With this realization comes the key to this new era, where some rather remarkable achievements await us. Let us look into that future with anticipation and excitement. And let us enter with the confidence these attributes afford. In the words of Kahlil Gibran: "Come, for only the coward tarries, and it is folly to look back on the City of the Past."